The State
of the Nation
and the Agenda
for Higher Education

✤✤✤✤ **Howard R. Bowen**

The State
of the Nation
and the Agenda
for Higher Education

Jossey-Bass Publishers

San Francisco • Washington • London • 1982

THE STATE OF THE NATION AND THE AGENDA FOR HIGHER EDUCATION
by Howard R. Bowen

Copyright © 1982 by: Jossey-Bass Inc., Publishers
433 California Street
San Francisco, California 94104
&
Jossey-Bass Limited
28 Banner Street
London EC1Y 8QE

Library of Congress Cataloging in Publication Data

Bowen, Howard Rothmann, 1908-
    The state of the nation and the agenda for
higher education.

    Bibliography: p. 195
    Includes index.
    1. Education, Higher—United States.
2. United States—Social conditions—1970-
3. Education, Higher—Aims and objectives.
I. Title.
LB2331.72.B68   378.73   81-20746
ISBN 0-87589-515-8   AACR2

Manufactured in the United States of America

JACKET DESIGN BY WILLI BAUM

FIRST EDITION

Code 8206

The Jossey-Bass
Series in Higher Education

Preface

✣✣✣✣

About fifty years ago, J. M. Keynes (1930) wrote a charming and perceptive essay on "Economic Possibilities for Our Grandchildren." He speculated that in the foreseeable future the intrinsic need of human beings for economic goods and services (as distinct from their use as symbols of status and power) might be satisfied in the sense that people would "prefer to devote their further energies to noneconomic purposes." Keynes concluded: "Assuming no important wars and no important increase in population, the *economic problem* may be solved, or be at least within sight of solution, within a hundred years. This means that the economic problem is not, if we look into the future, the *permanent problem of the human race*" (1930, p. 326). He then went on to sketch the implications of this "startling" conclusion. It would require people to adopt radically new lifetime values and unfamiliar patterns of behavior.

Since Keynes wrote this essay, his assumptions about war and population growth have not been realized. Yet, in the industrial nations at least, a level of production has been achieved—or is achievable—that could yield enough goods to satisfy easily the absolute needs of all their citizens. Perhaps in another fifty years, barring war

ix

and population growth, it would be possible for the whole world to achieve a level of abundance such as Keynes foresaw.

My purpose in this book is to speculate on the *educational* possibilities for our grandchildren in the same way that Keynes considered the economic possibilities. Education is, of course, linked closely to economic trends. Not only does it influence the rate of growth of production but also, through its effect on human values, it influences the way the product is distributed and used. But the influence of education extends far beyond the realm of economics. It is—or can be—a means of enhancing the personality of individuals. It can impart desirable personal qualities such as rationality, knowledge, tolerance, creativeness, moral awareness, esthetic sensibility, personal self-discovery, and human understanding. It can lead to practical competence in work and also in citizenship, family life, health and physical fitness, and leisure activities. Ultimately, education influences the kind of people our children and grandchildren will become; through them, it helps to form the kind of society they will live in. And so this book is addressed to these questions: What kind of people do we want our children and grandchildren to be? What kind of society do we want them to live in? How may education—especially higher education—be guided and shaped to help nurture such people and to help create this kind of society?

Questions such as these demand perspective of educators and public officials. They relate to goals and possibilities over several generations, not merely to imminent necessities such as financing next year's budget or recruiting next year's freshman class. Such questions force sights to be raised above the immediately practical to the distantly ideal. The intention is to find guidance for the current policies of institutions and government in the larger vision of what can be achieved and what ought to be achieved in the distant future.

Attention to the long-term possibilities for higher education may seem useless or even frivolous at a time when many colleges and universities are experiencing financial stringency, some are preoccupied with sheer survival, and all are apprehensive. Furthermore, even to consider future possibilities that may add to cost may seem futile and indiscreet at a time when the slashing of governmental civil budgets is the order of the day. But the concerns of the present do not necessarily carry over to the future. If there is one prediction for the future that is sure to be correct, it is that things will be different—perhaps in surprising ways. And so it is no act of futility and no lapse of discretion to ponder long-range possibilities and thus to help in the guidance of short-range decisions.

The book is divided into four sections of two chapters each. Chapters One and Two provide an appraisal of American higher education as it exists today. They briefly recount its history from World War II to 1981 and present evidence on the educational attainments of the American people today and in the foreseeable future.

The next two chapters are a study of "the state of the nation." Chapter Three is a survey of trends in the population, the economy, social conditions, communications, education, the arts and sciences, and the general quality of life. This survey, which includes an extended statistical appendix, is of interest in its own right as well as being relevant to education. It assembles a great deal of information—some of it surprising and contrary to general opinion—about the present condition of American society. Chapter Four reviews the major problems facing the nation and identifies the most important responsibilities of Americans.

Chapters Five and Six explore the place of education in a society characterized by political democracy and economic capitalism and examine the role of higher education as a catalyst for social change. Finally, Chapters Seven and Eight, building on the preceding analysis, identify several specific goals for higher education—goals that are of the utmost urgency and that should guide the policy of our colleges and universities over many decades. These goals are not new or unheard of, nor do they supplant the conventional objectives of higher education. They have been part of educational thinking for centuries. But they do call for new directions and changes of emphasis as colleges and universities prepare to play their parts in meeting the needs of a democratic society.

The book is directed primarily at educators in colleges and universities. Its message is also pertinent for those concerned with elementary and secondary education. But the basic question of how our children should be educated is also of interest to everyone—parents, public leaders who must decide on educational questions, trustees of educational institutions, concerned citizens, and, not least of all, students.

I acknowledge with appreciation the opportunity and freedom afforded by my appointment as a Fellow of The Carnegie Foundation for the Advancement of Teaching during the academic year 1980-81. The president of the foundation, Ernest L. Boyer, and his associates were generous with both their assistance and their criticisms. The ultimate responsibility for errors, omissions, and lapses of judgment lies, however, with me.

Claremont, California
September 1981

HOWARD R. BOWEN

Contents

Preface   ix

The Author   xvii

1. American Higher Education:
    Recent History and Present Condition   1

2. How Well-Educated Are the American People?   11

    Past Trends in Educational Attainment   •
    Projections of Future Educational Attainment   •
    Educational Content   •   *Findings from Studies
    of Competence, Knowledge, and Values*   •
    *Needed: A Periodic Survey of Educational
    Attainments*   •   *Conclusions*

3. Progress of the Nation   24

    The Population   •   *The Economy*   •   *Social*

Conditions • *Communications, Education,
Arts, and Science* • *Quality of Life* •
Conclusions

4. Problems Facing the Nation 54

Economic Problems • *Social Problems* •
Educational Problems • *Political Problems*
• *Conclusions: The Informed and Socially
Responsible Citizen and Leader* • *Conclusions:
The Plight of Youth*

5. Education in a Democracy 69

Equilibrium • *Economic Problems* •
Political Problems • *Values: The Missing
Ingredient* • *The Role of Education* •
Conclusions

6. Higher Education and Social Change 82

Sources of Influence • *Liberal Learning* •
What Can Be Done?

7. Toward a Nation of Educated People 99

The Baccalaureate Degree • *The Course of
Study* • *Characteristics of a Well-Educated
Person* • *Educability* • *What Would a
Nation of Educated People Be Like?*

8. Agenda for Higher Education 125

A Nation of Educated People • *Education for
Values* • *American Youth* • *International
Reconciliation* • *Concluding Comments*

Appendix A. Indicators of Economic and Social
Progress in the United States, 1950–1980 157

Contents

Appendix B. Data on the Educational Attainments
of the American People   187

Bibliography   195

Index   205

The Author   ✤✤✤✤

HOWARD R. BOWEN is R. Stanton Avery Professor of Economics and
Education at Claremont Graduate School. A native of Spokane,
Washington, he attended Washington State University, received the
Ph.D. degree in economics from the University of Iowa (1935), and
was a postdoctoral student at Cambridge University and the London
School of Economics (1937–1938). He is an economist who in recent
years has specialized in the economics of higher education.

His career has included service in business, government, and
higher education. Bowen was chief economist of the Joint Committee on Internal Revenue Taxation of the U.S. Congress (1942–1945)
and economist of the Irving Trust Company, a Wall Street bank
(1945–1947). He has taught at the University of Iowa, Williams
College, and Claremont Graduate School. He served as dean of the
Business School at the University of Illinois and as president or
chancellor of three institutions: Grinnell College (1955–1964), the
University of Iowa (1964–1969), and Claremont University Center
(1970–1974).

Bowen has served on the boards of many organizations and is
currently a director or trustee of Grinnell College, Claremont Uni-

versity Center, and Teachers Insurance and Annuity Association. He has been president of the American Finance Association, The American Association for Higher Education, the Association for the Study of Higher Education, and the Western Economic Association and chairman of the National Citizens' Committee for Tax Revision and Reduction (1963) and of the National Commission on Technology, Automation, and Economic Progress. He is a member of the National Academy of Education. Bowen has been a member of foreign missions to Japan, Thailand, and Yugoslavia. His numerous honorary degrees and awards include special awards for educational leadership presented by the National Council of Independent Colleges and Universities, the New York Association of Colleges and Universities, and *Change* magazine.

Howard Bowen is the author or coauthor of ten books and many articles and pamphlets. Among his books are *Toward Social Economy* (1948, reprinted 1977), *Social Responsibilities of the Businessman* (1953), *Graduate Education in Economics* (1954), *Automation and Economic Progress* (1966), *The Finance of Higher Education* (1969), *Efficiency in Liberal Education* (1971), *Investment in Learning* (1977), and *The Costs of Higher Education* (1981).

The State
of the Nation ✦✦✦✦
and the Agenda
for Higher Education

American Higher Education

1

❖❖❖❖

Recent History
and Present Condition

But consideration must be given to the question, what consti-
tutes education and what is the proper way to be educated. At
present there are differences of opinion as to the proper tasks to
be set; for all peoples do not agree as to the things that the
young ought to learn, either with a view to virtue or with a view
to the best life, nor is it clear whether their studies should be
regulated more with regard to intellect or with regard to charac-
ter. And confusing questions arise out of the education that
actually prevails, and it is not at all clear whether the pupils
should practice pursuits that are practically useful, or morally
edifying, or higher accomplishments.

—Aristotle, *Politics*, Book VIII

From the beginning of the American adventure, education occupied
a central position. As the nation grew in strength and resources, the
educational system was steadily widened by serving more people and
deepened by lengthening the years of study and improving educational standards. It was a fundamental article of faith that the
growth of education had been and would continue to be a major
source of economic and social progress. It was believed that educated
people were needed to serve the professions, to conduct the government, to lead the church and other social institutions, to carry on the
cultural life of the nation, to conceive and operate new technologies,
to conduct an industry and commerce of growing magnitude and

complexity, and to provide military leadership. It was also believed that substantial education was needed by the rank and file who would be the citizens, workers, farmers, soldiers, parents, and consumers. Throughout its history, America—by comparison with most countries—has provided abundant opportunities and incentives for the education of its people. Of course, American history is replete with brilliant leaders of limited formal education, Abraham Lincoln being the favorite example. Yet most of these persons were not uneducated. Rather, they were self-educated, and self-education was not without honor.

Since World War II, American higher education has had an eventful history and has continued to make substantial contributions to our national life. The postwar era, however, has not been a time of profound concern for purpose, or serious exploration of educational content, or of significant and lasting innovation in method. Rather, it has been a time of concentration on growth.

The concern for growth immediately after World War II, as reflected in the GI Bill, was based in part on gratitude to the returning war veterans, on the desire to prevent their unemployment, and on the widespread belief that education and basic research were essential to national economic development and military power. And these goals were soon reinforced by attitudes surrounding the cold war and the space race. Moreover, not long after the war, the attention of the American people began to drift toward egalitarian objectives. Partly as a result of the resounding success of the GI Bill, higher education was seen increasingly as a source of economic and social opportunity for individuals. An early manifestation of this tendency was the influential report of the President's Commission on Higher Education (1947). The idea spread rapidly that higher education should be available to all qualified persons regardless of family income, sex, ethnic origin, religion, or handicap. Thus, with the combined force of arguments based on economic growth and national power and arguments based on equality of opportunity, the drive for enrollment growth became irresistible and "access" became the dominating idea behind the development of higher education. As a result, billions of dollars of federal, state, and private funds flowed to higher education, some in the form of appropriations and gifts for institutional operations and capital and some in the form of student financial aid. Meanwhile, during the 1960s and 1970s, the growth of enrollment was fed by the postwar baby boom, which greatly increased the number of potential college students.

To accommodate the burgeoning student population, an unprecedented wave of institution building became necessary. Existing institutions were expanded, former teacher's colleges were converted into universities, and new institutions—especially community colleges—sprang up everywhere. More facilities were constructed and more staff added during this period than had been accumulated in the previous three centuries. In the 1970s, enrollments were further expanded, especially by a great influx of part-time and commuting students—some youthful and some beyond the traditional college age—who would not previously have attended when college had been reserved mainly for full-time residential students.

The net result of the postwar experience was one of the greatest achievements ever in the history of higher education, namely, the opening up of colleges and universities to a substantial portion of the traditional age cohorts and to millions of older persons as well. Through the achievements of the postwar period, higher education changed from a preserve of a privileged minority of the people to a place of personal development open to qualified persons of all classes. In the 1970s, however, the rate of enrollment growth slowed and near the end of that decade almost leveled out.

Meanwhile, the universities (and, to some extent, other types of institutions) were gearing up for an unprecedented expansion of research and scholarship, public service, and graduate study. They were financed in these efforts partly by the federal government, partly by private foundations and corporations, and partly by the institutions themselves as they reaped rewards from economies of scale and diverted resources from undergraduate instruction to research, public service, and graduate study.

The history of higher education over the past thirty years is epitomized in Table 1, which shows the increase in enrollments, number of institutions, and expenditures for organized research. The dominant feature of the table is growth based on vastly broadened access to higher education. This growth was accompanied by several noteworthy changes in the complexion of American higher education—changes that probably affected quality or performance.

**Table 1. Institutions of Higher Education: Estimated Number,
Enrollments, and Expenditures for Research and Development**

	1950	1960	1970	1980[e]
Number of institutions[a]				
Four-year	1,345	1,451	1,639	1,810
Two-year	518	508	886	1,030
Total	1,863	1,959	2,525	2,840
Enrollment (in millions)[b]				
All students	2.3	3.8	8.6	12.0
Full-time equivalents	2.1	2.9	6.7	9.0
Expenditures for organized research and development (billions of 1967 dollars)[c]	0.3[d]	0.7	2.0	2.2

[a] U.S. Bureau of the Census, *Historical Statistics of the United States* (1975, Vol. 1. p. 382); National Center for Education Statistics, *Digest of Education Statistics* (1980, p. 115).
[b] National Center for Education Statistics, *Digest of Education Statistics* (1980), pp. 87, 89).
[c] National Science Foundation (1977).
[d] 1953.
[e] Estimated by author.

One such change was a subtantial shift in the mixture of institutions resulting from the differential growth of the parts of the system. The public sector grew in the number of institutions and enrollment more rapidly than the private sector; two-year colleges grew more rapidly than four-year institutions. At the same time, the average size of institutions increased substantially. Another new departure was a pronounced change in the composition of the student population as the relative numbers of "nontraditional" students increased, among them part-time, low-income, minority, handicapped, older undergraduate, and graduate students. During the later 1970s, also, the academic ability of students as measured by scholastic aptitude tests declined, and the secondary school preparation of college-bound students sagged badly. It is perhaps fair to say that educators were not able to adjust fully to the needs of the new students, many of whom were from minority backgrounds, attended part time, and were nonresidential.

Still another change was the proliferation of curricula as new disciplines were admitted and the contents of many old ones were expanded. One aspect of this proliferation was the introduction of innumerable vocational programs by the community colleges and also, to a lesser extent, by the comprehensive four-year institutions. Meanwhile, the interests and aspirations of the faculties were gradually and subtly changing. Their interests tended to be more specialized and technical than those of their predecessors. Their aspirations came to be focused increasingly on achievements in research and scholarship within their specialties. Faculty members tended to see themselves as professional persons in narrow fields of research or study and to regard their role as teachers to be the transmittal of their particular specialties rather than the broad cultivation of students as persons. They were encouraged in these tendencies by a reward system that conferred the highest status and the most generous compensation on those who were outstanding achievers in research and scholarship. They were also encouraged by the expansion of federal support for academic research, which made possible an immense increase in the amount of basic research conducted in the major universities.

Two other developments, both relating to the autonomy of institutions, should be mentioned among the major changes in the postwar period. One of these was a palpable increase in political control. The explosive growth of American higher education meant that the educational system became so large, complex, and costly that some coordination and direction at the system level seemed inevitable. The federal government, having chosen to concentrate its support of higher education mainly on student financial aid and selective grants for research and public service, left the task of coordination largely to the states. However, the federal government used its considerable leverage to exert controls in various ways. All fifty of the states established coordinating bodies in the form of multicampus university systems or special state agencies. They also increased their oversight of higher education through legislative committees and finance officers and other representatives of the executive branch of state government. The result was tighter political and administrative control over higher education with gradual erosion of institutional autonomy. These controls affected public institutions more directly than private institutions, but the private institutions were not wholly immune.

A second development relating to autonomy was the growing power of students in the affairs of colleges and universities. This growth came about in part as a result of the organized student protests in the late 1960s. At that time, most colleges and universities retreated from their traditional responsibility, *in loco parentis,* for the private lives of their students. The practice of treating students as responsible adults became widespread. Moreover, at many colleges and universities, students were allowed or encouraged to take part in institutional policy making. Much more important than these changes, however, was the increasing role of students in the finances of both private and public institutions. In the case of private institutions, the proportion of total revenues derived from endowments declined drastically, and, with few exceptions, private colleges and universities became largely dependent for their income on tuitions and fees paid by students. In a different way, the public institutions also became heavily dependent on students. Their funds came to be derived partly from tuitions and fees and partly from state appropriations determined by formulas in which enrollment was the dominant factor. This relationship between enrollment and finances was cemented even more strongly when the federal government chose to support higher education through aid to students rather than aid to institutions. The finances of both private and public institutions, of course, had never been unrelated to enrollments. But in the distant past, the financial arrangements allowed some leeway to accommodate general institutional needs and some time for adjustment to changing enrollments. Today most institutions are in the position of almost immediate dependence upon the number of students for their financial sustenance; they live or die according to their ability to attract and retain students (Bowen, 1980b, Chap. 10). This shift in power toward students has been described in considerable detail by Riesman (1980). Under these conditions, the power of institutional leaders and their faculties to set the direction of their institutions— to decide on curricula, to establish standards, and to deploy resources—was eroded. Institutional policy came to be dictated by whatever attracts and holds students, and educational policy making was largely shifted to the market for students away from decisions based on the professional judgments of educators. Although student choices and professional decisions were not always at odds and the rise of student influence did, in some respects, yield important benefits, power did shift. In many institutions, educational practices and standards were compromised. Unfortunately, the shift in power happened to occur at a time when the job market for college graduates was weak. In this situation, student demand moved strongly toward vocational-professional education at the expense of general education. Also, the shift in power probably led institutions to soften their residence requirements with the result that many students who—from an educational point of view—could and should have been full-time residential students became part-time commuters.

With finances so closely linked to students, educators looked upon a possible decline in enrollment with dread. In recent years they became preoccupied with the impending decline in college-age cohorts and with ways to avoid shrinkage of their particular institutions. Higher educational discourse came to be riveted on "the outlook for the 1980s and 1990s" in terms of enrollments, finance, and institutional survival.

Most of the changes I have described were perhaps inevitable accompaniments of growth. Many of them would probably be regarded by most informed observers as unfavorable in their effect on educational quality, at best neutral, but nevertheless justifiable as part of the process of extending higher education to millions of new learners. During the postwar era, educators were not unmindful of quality. Their efforts to improve the performance of higher education were concentrated, however, largely on faculty and staff salaries and fringe benefits, the intention being to pay compensation sufficient to attract and retain personnel of first-rate competence. Compensation levels (in real terms) were raised dramatically during the period 1950 to 1970. Although some of the gains during that period were later eroded by inflation, the compensation levels prevailing in 1980 (in real dollars) were far higher than those of the early 1950s (Bowen, 1980b, chap. 3). The money spent on faculty and staff probably had its intended effect; higher education was almost certainly able to attract and hold personnel of higher ability than ever before, and in that critical respect institutional quality was raised.

Many innovations in method were attempted, for example, early admission, advanced placement, modified academic schedules, mechanically assisted instruction, independent study in many forms, competency based instruction, and external degrees. And various fads held sway briefly. But, on the whole, the conduct and style of higher education were not drastically different in 1980 from what they had been in 1950. (See Grant and Riesman, 1978, for a vivid account of the tribulations of experimental colleges during the postwar period.) The attention of educators was focused on growth and the problems associated with growth—or more recently with decline and the infinitely more tedious problems associated with decline. Their major concerns were recruitment and financial aid of students, recruitment and compensation of staff, provision of facilities, institutional organization, governance, cutting costs, and finance. Unintentionally, the emphasis undoubtedly shifted away from broad liberal learning to specialized, technical, and vocational education. The professional competence of the faculties probably improved. Among the major universities, relative emphasis on research increased. Influence in the policy and decisions of the institutions probably shifted from administrators and faculty to government and students, with students deriving increasing impact from their market power. Furthermore, the postwar era was not a particularly fruitful period for the discussion of educational philosophy. Some notable faculty reports and treatises on general education appeared, but remarkably little influential or enduring literature on education's purpose was written. There were few if any towering figures comparable to Newman, Dewey, or Whitehead. Rather, the thinking and discourse of educators was related primarily to bread-and-butter issues. The great questions of what kind of people they were trying to produce or what kind of society they hoped to achieve were left to conventional platitudes. Indeed, the thinking was resource oriented rather than outcome oriented. The pervasive belief was that if adequate resources were available, good education would automatically follow.

The 1980s are now upon us and higher education is in the doldrums. The range of possibilities is still vast. The number of persons of all ages in our society who are educable and who would be benefited by higher education vastly exceeds any past or present enrollment. The number who will in fact attend will depend on many variables, among them, the kind of education offered, its convenience in regard to time and place, admissions requirements, the amount and kind of student aid, the encouragement of employers, and so on. Moreover, any gap in enrollment might be filled by greater attention to quality, by expanded research and public service, and by a serious attack on the problems of the educationally disadvantaged. What happens will depend also on institutional and governmental initiative and policy. Maintaining the status quo and thus allowing enrollments to fall and precipitating a major depression in higher education is only one of the many options before the nation.

What is done in the 1980s and beyond should be guided not alone by expediency related to keeping the colleges and universities afloat but also by a larger vision of where higher education could and should be headed in the twenty-first century. This part of the discourse on the place of higher education in American society is strangely and tragically missing. If we had this larger and longer vision, most of the questions about the 1980s would be resolved. Educators would know what ought to be done in the near future and they would have a firm basis, other than maintaining the status quo or passively adapting to the market, for seeking support from society.

The questions to be asked are those I presented in the preface:

- What kind of people do we want our children and grandchildren to be?
- What kind of society do we want them to live in?
- How may higher education be guided and shaped to help nurture people of this kind and to help create this kind of society?

Higher education is, of course, not alone in the shaping of our people or in the shaping of our society. It shares these functions with the family, church, workplace, school, mass media, library, museum, peer group, social and political organizations, casual conversation, and even private thought and meditation. Thus, part of the question about the education of our grandchildren relates to the division of labor among these many educational institutions or media of which higher education is only one. However, the influence of higher education should not be overlooked or belittled. It now serves about a third to a half of every age cohort of young people and touches the lives of millions of other persons in less intensive encounters; it trains virtually the entire leadership of the society in the professions, government, business, and, to a lesser extent, the arts; more specifically, it trains the teachers, clergy, journalists, physicians, and others whose main function is the shaping and guiding of personal development; it is the principal locus of basic research and scholarship; it is the main custodian of the cultural heritage; it supports a great pool of faculty talent available to consult on almost every conceivable practical question; and, as a highly visible presence in our society, it continually communicates its values and its concerns to the general public. The influence may have expanded in recent decades with the growth of enrollments and with increasing participation of faculties in public affairs and private consulting. In other respects, this influence may have waned as the institutions have become larger and less personal, as the proportion of students attending full time and in residence has declined, and as the institution's role *in loco parentis* has diminished. Despite these shifts in the depth of its influence, higher education remains a social institution of great actual power and of even greater potential power. It is one of the levers by which a society can affect its destiny. Higher education can be consciously and deliberately used to help shape the trend of a national, or even world, culture. It is, of course, not strong enough to overpower all other influences bearing on cultural development, but it is strong enough to count.

How Well-
Educated Are the
American People?

2
❖ ❖ ❖ ❖

Our state of ignorance about the outcomes of education is not bliss.

—Alexander Astin
(From an address given at the University
of Texas on February 4, 1981).

From colonial days, education in America has been both an article of faith and a growth industry. The nation has steadily widened education by extending it to an ever larger percentage of the people, and deepened it by increasing, on the average, the years people spend in school and college. But what has been the result of all this effort to bring more education to more people? Just how well-educated are the American people today? And how well-educated are they likely to become in the foreseeable future? These are the questions to be addressed in this chapter.

In judging the educational attainments of the American people, one would like to find out what they know, what they can do, what they value, how they are motivated, and so on. Unfortunately, only the most meagre information of this kind is available, and so one must depend mainly on statistics about school and college attendance. Defining educational attainment in terms of attendance fails, of course, to take account of the substantial learning acquired without benefit of formal schooling and fails equally to allow for the considerable schooling that did not yield learning. Nevertheless, data relating to school attendance exist and, though not ideal for the purpose at hand, are instructive.

Past Trends in Educational Attainment

Over the years the educational attainment of the population has risen rapidly and steadily. Table 2 presents data gathered by the U.S. Bureau of the Census on years of school and college completed by adult Americans twenty-five years old or over. The table shows a steady decline in the percentage of adults whose education was limited to the grade school level, a steady increase in the percentage of persons who have graduated from high school, and a threefold

Table 2. Percentage of Population 25 Years Old and Over, by Years of School or College Completed, 1940-1979

Years of School and College Completed	1940[a]	1950[a]	1960[b]	1970[a]	1979[c]
Elementary					
0-4	13.7%	11.2%	8.3%	5.3%	3.5%
5-7	17.4[d]	15.1[d]	13.8	9.1	6.2
8	29.3[d]	22.1[d]	17.5	13.4	8.6
Subtotal	60.4	48.4	39.6	27.8	18.3
High school					
1-3	15.2	17.5	19.2	17.1	14.0
4	14.3	20.7	24.6	34.0	36.6
Subtotal	29.5	38.2	43.8	51.1	50.6
College					
1-3	5.5	7.3	8.8	10.2	14.7
4 or more	4.6	6.1	7.7	11.0	16.4
Subtotal	10.1	13.4	16.5	21.2	31.1
Total	100.0	100.0	100.0	100.0	100.0
Median school years completed	8.4	9.3	10.6	12.2	12.5

[a] U.S. Bureau of the Census, *Statistical Abstract of the United States* (1953, p. 115; 1964, p. 113; 1980, p. 149).
[b] *Statistical Abstract* (1975, p. 118).
[c] *Statistical Abstract* (1980, p. 149)
[d] Author's estimate.

increase in the percentage who have attended college. The median years of school attended increased from 8.4 in 1940 (just above the grade school level) to 12.5 in 1979 (just above the high school level), a net gain of four years.

As one considers the data for 1979, however, it is surprising to learn that 18.3 percent (almost one fifth) of the population did not attend beyond grade school and that only 16.4 percent had graduated from college.

Projections of Future Educational Attainment

The educational attainments of the present adult population are, of course, a resultant from the educational system and the rates of participation as they existed in the past, not as they exist today. To discover the consequences of the educational system as it exists today, it is necessary to project the educational attainments of the population into the distant future. For this purpose, I shall make three assumptions: (1) that the higher educational system continues without change just as it was constituted in 1979, (2) that the rates of participation also remain unchanged, and (3) that one age cohort after another, beginning with the people born in 1980, pass through the given educational system until—perhaps by the year 2040—the great majority of the adult population will have been the products of this system. With these assumptions, one can estimate the educational attainments of the population that would flow from the educational system as it now exists. The estimate for 2040, with comparative figures for 1979, is shown in Table 3.

The most striking feature of the table is the estimated large decline in the percentage of adults with only a grade school education. Nearly all children in the United States now attend grade school. In the mid-twenty-first century, therefore, only a small residue, 2 percent of the adult population, would be without at least a grade school education.

Another significant feature of Table 3 is the projected increase in the percentage of persons whose education would end in the first three years of high school. This group comprises many of the people who in an earlier generation would have been among those with only a grade school education.

Table 3. Estimated Percentage of the Population 25 Years and Older,
by Years of School or College Completed, 1979 and 2040

Years of School and College Completed	Actual 1979[a]	Estimated 2040 (assuming that educational system and rates of participation remain unchanged from 1980 on)[b]
Elementary		
0–4	3.5%	0.5%
5–7	6.2	0.5
8	8.6	1.0
Subtotal	18.3	2.0
High school		
1–3	14.0	24.0
4	36.6	27.0
Subtotal	50.6	51.0
College		
1–3	14.7	19.0
4 or more	16.4	28.0
Subtotal	31.1	47.0
Total	100.0	100.0

[a] U.S. Bureau of the Census, *Statistical Abstract of the United States* (1980, p. 149).

[b] Rough estimates based on many sources, especially, National Center for Education Statistics, *Digest of Education Statistics* (1980, pp. 6–10, 63, 65, 88, 95–96, 112–116, 118, 123, 148–149); National Center for Education Statistics, *Projections of Education Statistics to 1986–87* (1980, pp. 20–25); U.S. Bureau of the Census, *Statistical Abstract of the United States* (1979, pp. 139–148).

The projected decline in the percentage of those whose education would end with the fourth year of high school may be explained by the increasing college attendance of high school graduates. In 1979, the percentage of the adult population who had attended college was 31.1 percent; this percentage is projected to be 47 percent in 2040—almost half the population. In 1979, the percentage who had graduated from college was 16.4 percent; the estimated figure for the year 2040 is 28.0 percent—over a quarter of the population.

From these estimates it is clear that the education system as it now exists would, if continued unchanged over the next sixty years, produce a substantial rise in the educational status of the American people. There would be relatively fewer persons with only elementary education, and many more with higher education. The population would be divided into four roughly equal groups; grade school only or high school dropouts (26 percent), high school graduates (27 percent), college attenders who did not receive bachelor's degrees (19 percent), and college graduates (28 percent). The estimates in Table 3 also indicate that the percentage not attending college would decline from 69 percent in 1979 to 53 percent in 2040, and the percentage attending college would increase from 31 to 47 percent.

If no further changes in participation rates occur, these figures suggest a slow but significant advancement in the formal education of the American people over the next sixty years. They also suggest that the nation is a long way from reaping the full benefits of the recent expansion of higher education. Because the returns to investments in education materialize only over the lifetimes of the people being educated, many decades must come and go before this expansion can be translated into educational attainments for the whole adult population. The process could, however, be short circuited by expansion of adult learning. Indeed, adult learning, which gives opportunity to those who would otherwise be passed up by the educational system, would thus hasten the process of raising the educational level of the population.

The figures in Table 3 are based on the assumptions of no change in the educational system and in the rates of participation. This assumption is, of course, not likely to be borne out in fact. The character of the educational system might change in many ways, for example, in the intensity and quality of the education provided, in the relative emphasis on vocational and general education, in the relative amount of education occurring within settings other than school and college, and in the instructional technologies employed. Similarly, the rates of participation might vary as a result of changes in the ethnic composition of the population, in the job market, in popular attitudes toward education, and in policies toward tuition, student aid, and admissions standards. The range of possibilities for future enrollments is very great. On the one hand, there will be plenty of people in need of additional education to justify substantial expansion; on the other hand, restrictive attitudes and policies toward education may result in contraction.

Educational Content

The character of the present educational system may be partially described in terms of student enrollments as between vocational and other programs. Relevant data are shown in Appendix Table B1.

Generally, the curricula of the first several years of elementary education are devoted to the three r's and to nonvocational subjects such as history, geography, music, art, and rudimentary science. Vocational subjects appear at about grade seven and gradually become more prominent. In high school, nearly half of all students are enrolled in academic or college preparatory programs and about a quarter are in vocational programs. However, when the intermediate category, the general course, is taken into account, it is probable that as many as one third of all high school students are in vocational programs.

Among entering full-time college freshmen, three fourths indicate that they are looking ahead to vocational majors. If part-time freshmen had been included in these figures, the proportion of prospective vocational majors would probably have been even greater. At the baccalaureate stage, the division is 61 percent vocational majors to 39 percent nonvocational. If two-year college students and dropouts from four-year colleges had been included in these figures, the proportion of vocational majors would doubtless have been substantially higher, perhaps more than two thirds.

Finally, adult education is widely diffused among various fields and interests, somewhat less than half in vocational training. Much of the rest, however, is of a practical nature related to the household, the family, and recreation, and it is safe to say that three fourths of adult education could be classified as practical if not vocational education.

The figures presented in Appendix Table B1 are suggestive, certainly not definitive. The classification of subjects or programs is of questionable validity. Reality may be quite different from appearances. Seemingly vocational subjects may be in fact quite liberal in spirit, and seemingly liberal subjects may be either vocational in spirit or narrowly pedantic. Nevertheless, from these data one gains the impression that from the seventh grade onward vocational instruction occupies a significant and increasing proportion of the school and college instruction and that in college vocational instruction is about two thirds of the total.

Findings from Studies of Competence, Knowledge, and Values

Investigations into the actual educational attainments of the adult population—expressed in terms of what they can do, what they know, and what they value—are exceedingly rare. Some information, derived from scores on standardized tests and other sources, is available on learning and on personality changes during school and college (Bowen, 1977, chaps. 3–7). There are also a few studies of the effect of formal education in school and college on the characteristics of adults. For example, Pace (1972, 1974, 1979) measured the educational outcomes of higher education by asking large samples of alumni about the benefits they had received from college. Economists have made numerous studies of the economic returns to investments in education or of the role of education in national economic growth (Douglass, in Bowen, 1977, chap. 12). Generally, studies of these kinds have shown that learning, desirable personality change, and economic productivity occur as a result of formal education and that the greater the amount of education the greater the effect. These studies usually show also that investments in education, at least through college, on the average produce returns that amply justify the cost. These studies, however, do not provide information on the competence, knowledge, and values of the entire adult population; they simply confirm that desirable characteristics are correlated with the amount of formal education. A few studies, however, provide some direct information on the competence, knowledge, and values of the adult population.

In one such study, a team of scholars at the University of Texas under the leadership of Norvell Northcutt conducted a nationwide survey of the ability of people to function in daily life.

This survey, known as the Adult Performance Level Study, was conducted with a carefully selected sample of the entire adult population. The principal results are shown in Appendix Table B2. The respondents were divided into three groups using criteria established through special studies: (1) those judged to be severely limited in functional competence, (2) those able to function with minimal adequacy, and (3) those deemed to be proficient. The data suggest that around half of the adult population are "proficient" in carrying on the various activities involved in daily living and working, a third function with "minimal adequacy," and a fifth are "severely limited" in their functional competence. Proficiency is strongly correlated with the level of formal education. Only a few of those with meagre education attain proficiency, and conversely, only a few of those with college education are classed as severely limited.*

Hunter and Harman (1979, p. 56) reviewed the Northcutt study and other investigations relating to learning deficiencies, especially illiteracy, and concluded:

> One fact emerges clearly from all the statistical information available, whether the measure is competency or school completion. Despite the universal free education available in this country since early in the century, despite the fact that more and more young people of all races and ethnic groups are completing high school, and despite the recent evidence that those who do complete high school are achieving "acceptable" levels of literacy, a disproportionately large section of our adult population—well over a third—still suffers some educational disadvantage (Fisher, 1978). Among these millions of adults in our society are the functionally illiterate. Their exact number is not known.
> We conclude that the aggregate message of all the statistics is more important than their specific accuracy. A much larger proportion of the U.S. population than had until

*An earlier study (Harris and Associates, 1971) concluded that about 15 percent of all adults have serious reading deficiencies. Another study (Kozol, 1980, p. 6) reviewed various sources of data and concluded that about 25 million adults, or 16 percent of the adult population, "lacked the skills to function at all." For an interesting definition of *illiteracy* see Kozol (1980, pp. 53–55).

recently been known or assumed suffers serious disadvantage because of limited educational attainment. In this country persons with limited education are often the same persons who suffer from one or more of the other major social disadvantages—poverty, unemployment, racial or ethnic discrimination, social isolation. Inadequate education will probably be only one manifestation of their deprivation. The greater the number of those disadvantages, the more serious the suffering for members of our society in which one's worth is judged by one's job, possessions, and credentials.

The findings of the Northcutt study and the conclusions of Hunter and Harman are quite different from those reported by the U.S. Bureau of the Census, which show that illiteracy has been falling steadily from 11.3 percent of the population in 1900 to 1.2 percent in 1970 (U.S. Bureau of the Census, *Statistical Abstract of the United States,* 1980, p. 150). Obviously, the definitions followed by the Bureau of the Census are much less rigorous than those adopted by the other investigators. The census data do indicate, however, that the spread of education has had the effect of reducing illiteracy as the bureau defines it. However, one cannot be sure that comparable progress has been made in reducing functional incompetence. As society becomes more complex over time, the level of competence required of individuals if they are to cope and compete rises steadily. Education for competency seems to be aimed toward a moving target. This is illustrated by recent reports from the armed forces to the effect that many enlisted men and women, who would have been competent military personnel in an earlier generation, lack the education needed to cope with military equipment of increasing sophistication.

A second source of information on the educational attainments of the adult population is the National Assessment of Educational Progress.* This organization makes periodic studies of the educational attainments of children of various ages and also of

*The National Assessment of Educational Progress is conducted by the Education Commission of the States, 1860 Lincoln Street, Denver, Colo. 80295. The studies are scattered among numerous publications, for example, *Consumer Math: Selected Results from the First National Assessment of Mathematics,* June 1975.

young adults between the ages of twenty-six and thirty-five. The main purpose of these studies is to trace changes in educational attainments over time, but some of the data provide information on the percentage of persons who are able to give correct answers to simple but practical questions relating to "consumer math," health, career planning, and other areas. The percentage of young adults choosing the correct responses generally varies from 40 to 80 percent. But, on the average, about one third of the respondents answer the various questions incorrectly.

Another source of information about the educational attainments of the adult population is contained in two studies by Herbert Hyman and his associates, one on what people know (Hyman, Wright, and Reed, 1975) and the other on what people value (Hyman, 1979). Both of these studies are based on data obtained from public opinion surveys. They were intended to show the relationship between the level of people's formal education and their knowledge and values, but the same data can be reclassified to provide information on the percentage of the adult population who give or fail to give the "correct" or "preferred" answers. Doubtless, many polls taken in future years could be reanalyzed for the purpose of discovering what people know and what they value. A sampling of data from the Hyman studies is shown in Appendix Tables B3 and B4. These figures suggest (with considerable variance) that a large minority of the population answered the factual questions incorrectly or chose "nonliberal" responses to questions on human rights.

The studies cited lead to the suspicion, if not the proof, that a substantial proportion of the American population has serious learning disabilities.

Needed: A Periodic Survey of Educational Attainments

The data reviewed in this chapter reveal less about the actual educational attainments of adult Americans than about the need for more knowledge of the subject. Minimal information is available on the percentage of adults who have reached various rungs on the formal educational ladder. A little is known about present-day attendance at school and college, enrollments by subject, and certificates and degrees awarded. From these data, the number of persons who will probably achieve various levels at specified dates in the future can be deduced. But information is minuscule on the actual competence, knowledge, and values of the adult population.

The learning that people acquire is by no means fully reflected in school and college transcripts. Their education also comes, during childhood, from the family, the church, the neighborhood, and the media. During adult life, it comes from all of these and also from the workplace, military service, travel, and virtually all other lifetime experiences. What is needed, therefore, is not merely information on time spent in attendance at school and college, or credentials earned, but actual competence, knowledge, and values acquired in any way whatsoever. And the information should reflect what has been omitted or forgotten from formal education and what has been learned from sources other than formal education. When one considers the size of the nation's commitment to education and the importance attached to the development of its people, it seems the height of irresponsibility not to know more than we do about the overall educational attainments of the population.

I suggest that a recurrent study should be conducted every five or ten years to discover what people know, what they can do, and what they value. The data gathered would be supplemented by information on their socioeconomic backgrounds and also by detailed data on their educational histories, including not only formal schooling but also education derived from such sources as self-education. The survey would, of course, be conducted by means of small samples of the population. The objective would be to obtain periodically an educational profile of the adult population as an indicator of the rate of progress in the educational attainments of the American people, as a window on the strengths, weaknesses, and blind spots in the educational system, and as a guide to educational policy.

The survey would aim to provide information on verbal and quantitative skills and proficiency in subjects commonly included in general education. It would provide information on skills or knowledge related to practical affairs such as vocations, interpersonal relations, personal business, child development, health, consumer choice, and use of leisure. And the survey would seek information on behaviors and attitudes that would reveal values.

Admittedly, this is an ambitious proposal. It would tax the abilities of specialists in the field of survey research. But it is not impossible, especially if the task were begun with very small samples and expanded over the years as experience accumulated. But, ambitious or not, the kind of periodic survey proposed is urgently needed if the nation is to have adequate knowledge of the outcomes of its overall educational system—including not only its schools and colleges but also its other institutions and other experiences that bear upon the formation of human personalities. Information of this kind would also help in learning about the effects on human development of different kinds of formal education and in that way would help guide public and institutional policy relating to our schools and colleges.

Conclusions

Data on the actual attainments or competency of the American people (as distinct from the amount of time they served in the formal educational system) are rare. From the few studies available, one would guess that somewhat more than half of the adult population are proficient in coping with the ordinary problems of life and that perhaps a third are seriously disadvantaged educationally.

What can one make of these inadequate scraps of information about the present and prospective future educational attainments of the American people? Unquestionably the nation has made considerable progress. And, given the present educational system, it can anticipate considerably more progress over the next sixty years. Whether it should be content with things as they are or should be pushing on to greater educational accomplishments would depend on a value judgment and a technical judgment. The value judgment would pertain to the question of how important it is to provide the opportunity and the encouragement for all people to develop themselves to the full extent of their potential. The technical judgment would pertain to the question of what proportion of the people are educable in the sense that they could benefit from substantially more education. With a relaxed attitude about the importance of personal development, and with a technical judgment that formal education has already been pushed to near the limit, the decision would be perhaps to consolidate past gains and to maintain the educational system in approximately its present form and scope. On the other hand, with a strong belief in the importance of personal development and with a judgment that large numbers of people are potentially educable well beyond present attainments, the decision would be to push on toward both the widening and deepening of education. The objective would be to leave substantially fewer people on the lower rungs of the educational ladder and help substantially more to reach the upper rungs. These judgmental and technical questions will be considered in later chapters where the unequivocal conclusion is that education in increasing amounts could and should be extended to a vastly larger proportion of the population. Meanwhile, we shall turn to a consideration of the current condition of American society as related to the future responsibilities of higher education.

Progress
of the Nation

3

✤✤✤✤

Any fruitful reflection about the purposes of education must now begin with a definition of our own social and cultural condition. We shall need to ask what our world is like and what it needs.

—William J. Bouwsma (in Kaplan, 1980, p. 27)

Men are upset, not by events, but rather by the way they view them.

—Epictetus, *The Enchiridion V*

The purpose of this book is to consider the long-range opportunities and obligations of higher education to enhance life in America. This purpose calls for an appraisal of the state of the nation as it has evolved over the past several decades and identification of the major problems it will be facing in the decades ahead. In this chapter the progress of American society since World War II will be reviewed by a detailed examination of statistics. In the following chapter, an effort will be made to interpret the postwar historical record, to identify successes and failures, and to discover the leading problems. From this effort, the more urgent agenda of the nation may become visible and the responsibilities of higher education may to some extent be clarified (see Dewey, "The School and Society" in Archambault, 1964).

A review of the progress of the nation, as presented in this chapter, is of interest in its own right aside from its relevance to the future of higher education. The state of the nation is so often described in terms of the huge generalities of political debate, of journalistic hyperbole, or of social criticism that a sober factual review of underlying trends may be edifying and may indeed lead to surprising conclusions.

24

The American people stand today at what many believe to be a critical turning point in their social development. Historically, they have lived through the struggle for independence, the opening up of a continent, the unfolding of a fabulously productive economy, and a long series of military successes. They have achieved social and cultural progress on many fronts. True, the pace of development has been uneven, but the powerful underlying trends have been those of progress as measured by growth and improvement. The prevailing mood of the country has been that of pride in past achievements and optimism for the future. America has represented a fresh start for mankind through a new and superior civilization in the New World. And it has been accepted almost as dogma that the United States is a model for other nations to emulate.

Today the historic confidence, optimism, and drive of the American people may have diminished. There is a prevailing sense that the government, the economy, and other social institutions are not working well, that America is losing its influence in the world and its sense of destiny, that it may be entering a phase of decadence and decline. The malaise has doubtless been accentuated by a long series of "hard knocks" and disturbing events or conditions, among them, the assassinations of American leaders, the unleashing of nuclear energy, racial violence, student revolts, the Vietnam War, Watergate, the development of the Organization of Petroleum Exporting Countries (OPEC), the taking of American hostages, the endless succession of dangerous Middle Eastern crises, rampant inflation, unemployment, and crime.

The mood of pessimism happened to follow an enormous expansion of higher education, which was especially rapid in the period from 1955 to 1975. This higher educational boom was propelled by promises and hopes that it would lead to a richer civilization, a more bountiful economy, a militarily stronger nation, and generally a better life. From the perspective of the early 1980s, it appears to many that these promises and hopes have not been fulfilled. From many Americans' viewpoint, civilization has become decadent, the moral fiber of the people has decayed, the economy has been working badly, the military posture of the nation has deteriorated, and life has become harder and less satisfying. Higher education seems not to have been the panacea that had been promised.

To what extent are the gloomy attitudes of people about the nation's recent history actually justified by the facts? Which of the actual trends are adverse and which are favorable? Which impressions are factually valid and which are false? It is particularly important for educators to consider these questions because the answers will help to identify important national agenda for the future and to discern in what ways higher education may best contribute to social progress.

Appraising the state of the union is far from an exact science. Key data for the purpose are missing, and different observers place different interpretations on available information. However, it is possible to assemble many statistical indicators and other information to undergird judgments about the economic, social, and cultural condition of the country. In interpreting these data, however, five important qualifications must be considered.

First, a reasonably long view is essential: One should not be unduly influenced by the latest turn of events or the most recent crisis. It is necessary to study underlying and persistent trends and not merely dwell on incidents such as the latest wiggle in the trend of production or the outcome of the latest national election.

Second, the growth or progress of a nation along any particular dimension tends to be more rapid in the early stages of the nation's development than in the later stages. At the outset, growth or progress takes off from a very low base and can proceed at a rapid rate. As it goes on, however, more of the potential growth will have been exploited and further gains will become increasingly difficult to attain. Finally, a point will be reached at which further gains become slow, difficult, and costly. This pattern of development may be illustrated by an indicator such as human longevity. In the early stages of sanitation and the medical arts, when the average age at death may have been thirty years, there were many ready and inexpensive ways to improve sanitation and health care. Dramatic improvements were comparatively easy and cheap to attain. But after years of progress, when the average age at death has crept up to seventy or more, further gains are costly and difficult. The United States of today is a mature nation that has achieved enormous development in many ways and cannot be expected to sustain historic rates of progress indefinitely. True, radically new technologies sometimes give a sudden lift to the rate of development, but as these technologies are exploited, the rate again tends to subside. A slowing of the rate of development in a society can be a mark of success and maturity rather than an indicator of retrogression. In view of the effect of maturity on national development, comparisons among nations in the rate of development are not always meaningful.

Third, many of the problems of our society are not peculiar to the United States, but are common to all or most highly industrialized societies. Just as America has reached an exceptionally high point on the rising curve of industrialization, it has also reached a correspondingly high point on the curve of the particular social problems that are associated with industrialization. As an observer in Australia remarked, "Your present is our future" (Bronfenbrenner, 1980, p. 3). In the same vein, as a nation exploits a particular mode of achievement or progress (in America's case, industrialization), ennui sets in, and there is need for fresh goals and new adventures. Too often this need is fulfilled by war. What is called for just now in America is William James's "moral equivalent of war."

Fourth, in the study of economic and social development in the United States, it is important to rely, so far as possible, on objective data rather than mere opinion. However, objective data do not reflect all aspects of the underlying economic, social, and cultural trends, and so it is inevitable that, in the end, the state of the nation must be appraised in part by means of subjective judgments.

Fifth and finally, in appraising the conditions of the present, it is well to be cautious about idealizing the conditions of the past. People have a persistent tendency to look upon the past as a golden age and to overlook its flaws and weaknesses.

The remainder of this chapter is a review of statistical indicators and other information and analyses reflecting trends in the progress of the nation over the period from 1950 to 1980. The text is supported by the detailed statistical Appendix A, which contains a series of easy-to-read tables that speak for themselves. Whenever possible, the data are expressed in "real" terms, that is, they are corrected for inflation and population growth. Chapter Four contains a general interpretation of the data and identifies the agenda for the nation suggested by the facts.

The Population

The total population of the United States has been growing and is expected by the Bureau of the Census to continue to grow at least through the first half of the twenty-first century. (For detailed statistics related to this section, see Appendix Table A1.) The rate of growth, however, has declined substantially since 1950 and may be expected to level off in the twenty-first century. Also, the composition of the population by age has changed since 1950. The percentage of younger persons under eighteen increased until about 1960 and then declined sharply and is expected to decline further in the future. Meanwhile, the percentage of persons sixty-five and over has increased slowly but steadily since 1950 and is expected to increase further. Much has been made of this rising proportion of the elderly because it has been assumed that they will become a progressively increasing burden on the working population. This fear, however, overlooks a corresponding decline in the proportion of persons under the age of eighteen. In fact, the overall dependency index, measured by the percentage of the total population not of working ages, has been declining and is not expected to increase during the balance of this century.

Another significant change has been the increase in the proportion of the population resident in metropolitan areas. The great transformation from a rural and small town nation to a predominantly urban society has been largely completed and recently a reverse trend is in evidence. Today, nearly three quarters of the population live in metropolitan areas. Still another important development (not shown in Table A1) has been the change in the ethnic composition of the population, due partly to immigration and partly to differential birthrates among various elements of the population. The percentage of blacks increased from 9.9 percent in 1950 to 11.7 percent in 1980. The percentage of persons of Spanish origin grew rapidly to 6.4 percent in 1980. The percentage of people of Asian origins also grew substantially over recent decades.

A consequence of population growth combined with urbanization is that the scale of the organizations through which the society functions has been steadily increasing. Cities and towns, state and federal agencies, businesses, schools and colleges, and many other organizations are vastly larger than they were only a few decades ago. The result may be greater impersonality in everyday relationships, the spread of bureaucratic procedures, increasing anonymity, and loss of a sense of control of individuals over their own lives.

The Economy

Production. Production, like the weather, is subject to cyclical change and seldom follows a smooth path. (See Appendix Tables A2 and A3.) However, the underlying trend of production and productivity (expressed per capita and in constant dollars or physical units) has been strongly and persistently upward since 1950 (Table A2). Indeed, the period since that year has been one of the longest eras of basic economic stability and growth in American history. The experience in this period might tempt one to believe that the traditional scourge of recurrent deep depression has been overcome— though the sudden switch in economic philosophy and policy beginning around 1980 suggests caution in adopting any such belief.

The total gross national product (GNP) has been steadily rising since 1950, but the composition of the national product has undergone considerable change. As shown in Table A3, there has been a pronounced shift from the production of physical goods (agriculture, construction, and manufacturing) to the production of services (transportation, trade, finance, government, entertainment, repairs, and so on). These trends have been going on for many decades. Comparable trends are revealed in the breakdown of the GNP by type of product. As the GNP has grown, the American people have allocated an increasing proportion of their resources to durable goods (such as appliances and automobiles) and to services (such as entertainment, finance, and repairs), and a decreasing proportion to nondurable necessities (such as food and clothing). The changes in the composition of the GNP reflect the kind of economic change expected of a nation that is becoming increasingly affluent. Note, however, that during the past thirty years, the international economic position of the United States has deteriorated slightly as measured by U.S. assets held abroad relative to foreign assets in the United States (see Table A4).

Contrary to widespread opinion, the proportion of the GNP devoted to government has not expanded drastically (Table A3). Federal purchases of goods and services as a percentage of the GNP grew during the period of the Korean War, but have since been on a consistently downward trend. State and local outlays as a percentage of the GNP grew steadily until 1975, but have since been falling. Combined government purchases of goods and services (federal, state, and local) have been slowly declining relative to the GNP since 1970 (see Beck, 1976). These figures relate to the activities and operations of government. They do not include transfer payments such as payments to veterans, Medicaid patients, or Social Security annuitants. When transfer payments are included, government expenditures as a percentage of the GNP increased from 21 percent in 1950 to 34 percent in 1975, but declined since 1975 to 31 percent (Table A3). The upward trend occurred when the United States was concentrating on improving the well-being and the security of the less privileged.

The economic gains of the postwar era have been highlighted by Walter Heller (1980a): "the United States still stands head and shoulders above the rest of the world" in its standard of living; "the American worker is still the most productive in the world"; "the rise in U.S. labor costs is the slowest in the world"; from 1977 to 1980, "the volume of U.S. exports increased one third, considerably faster than the overall volume of world trade": "the dollar is rising in relation to other currencies: only in Australia and Japan do governments spend a smaller percentage of gross domestic product [GDP] than the 34 percent spent by our federal, state, and local governments in this country"; "and as to that 'crushing burden of taxes,' only Japan among our major competitors came in below the U.S. figure of 29 percent of GDP"; government spending has been declining: "Of the seven leading industrial countries, the United States has had the lowest ratio of overall government deficits to GNP"; even during the 1970s "per capita real income rose 23 percent." Heller concludes, "The battle to regain our economic momentum and subdue inflation will be long and tough. But no country can draw upon greater underlying strengths than the United States in fighting that battle."

A basic issue confronting the nation, however, is whether it would be expedient to push on toward even higher production— devoted to material gratification and achieved at the expense of depleting natural resources and fouling the environment—or whether it would be better to turn some of the nation's energies toward the increasing attainment of cultural excellence and human well-being. Opinion has been divided on this issue. But the long-run implications of unrestrained economic growth are so appalling that opinion must ultimately favor cultural excellence and human well-being over traditional economic objectives. No nation ever became or remained great by fixation on economic and military goals to the neglect of human and cultural attainments.

The Labor Force. The most striking feature of trends in the labor force over the past thirty years has been the huge increase in the number of participants as the postwar babies reached working age and as throngs of women took jobs outside the home. (See Appendix Tables A5 and A6.) From 1950 to 1980, more than 40 million people were added to the labor force. The growth was particularly rapid during the 1970s when the number of participants increased by over 20 million in a single decade. Amazingly, 38 million new jobs were created during this same period and unemployment increased by only 2 million. Indeed, it was not surprising that the rate of unemployment, which had been running 4 to 5 percent in the 1950s and 1960s, would increase in the face of the avalanche of new workers—both young people and women. Though no one can be satisfied with the unemployment rates of 6 to 9 percent, the increase in employment during the 1970s was a spectacular achievement of the American economy.

The incidence of unemployment has been especially severe among youthful workers as shown in Table A5 and also in the following figures for 1978 on unemployment rates by age of workers:

Age	Male	Female
16-19	15.7%	17.0%
20-24	9.1	10.1
25-34	4.3	6.7
35-44	2.8	5.0
45-54	2.8	4.0
55-64	2.7	3.2
65 and over	4.2	3.8

*U.S. Bureau of the Census, *Statistical Abstract of the United States* (1979, p. 396).

Indeed, the unemployment rates for persons of middle age have been almost irreducibly low.

The unemployment rate of the United States for all age groups combined has long been higher than ideal. It has seldom fallen below 3 or 4 percent except in times of war and is consistently higher than that in some other industrial countries. Some of this relatively high unemployment in the United States may be explained by the procedures and definitions used in compiling the statistics and some may be ascribed to the exceptional mobility of the American population. But some is doubtless due to the presence in the population of substantial numbers of persons who are only marginally employable because of disadvantaged backgrounds or who are left out because of discrimination.

Another remarkable trend over the past thirty years has been the change in the composition of the labor force by sex (Table A5). The number of men as a percentage of the total has been declining. Increasing numbers of younger men have been delaying entry to pursue education and increasing numbers of older men have been retiring before the traditional retirement age. The male percentage has, however, stabilized in recent years and it may increase under new retirement policies. Meanwhile, the percentage of women who have entered the labor force has exploded—an increase from 34 to 51 percent of women sixteen years of age and over. Because the entry of women has more than offset the decline in male participation, the combined labor force has grown relative to the population. The increase in the number of women in the labor force has occurred among single, widowed, and divorced women, but has been especially pronounced among married women. This change, of course, has had major implications for the family and for the welfare of children.

Impressive changes have also occurred over the past three decades in the distribution of the labor force by type of work (Table A6). These changes have been extensions of long-term trends, including a steady decline in the percentage of blue-collar and farm workers and a major increase in the percentage of white-collar and service workers. The percentage of white-collar workers grew from 37 to 51 percent of the total—to more than half of all workers. The professional, technical, managerial, and administrative workers alone now make up more than one fourth of the entire work force. These shifts are of enormous significance for higher education.

The Standard of Living. From the facts on the incomes, expenditures, and material possessions of the American people, one can only conclude that the American standard of living has improved steadily and substantially over the past thirty years. (See Appendix Tables A7, A8, A9, and A10.) Average family income in constant dollars almost doubled. And expenditure patterns changed in ways one would expect in a population that was becoming richer. The percentage spent on necessities such as food and clothing declined sharply, and the percentages spent on items that are more discretionary (housing, medical care, transportation, and recreation) increased. From a different perspective, the percentage spent on services increased from 39 to 46 percent while the percentage spent on physical goods decreased from 61 to 54 percent. Also, there was a steady upward trend in the percentage of owner-occupied housing units, in the average size of dwellings—despite a concurrent decline in family size, and in the amount and variety of household equipment. Perhaps the most spectacular change in the standard of living was the increased provision for leisure activities and recreation. This expansion was encouraged by changes in the allocation of time, including three-day weekends and paid vacations of increasing length.

In appraising the rise in the standard of living, one must recognize that some of it may have been achieved at a cost in the form of reduced consumer services, lower quality and durability of products, harmful ingredients, and increased risk of accidents. Furthermore, the sheer growth of population and the proliferation of physical goods have tended to impair satisfactions through congestion, litter, lack of privacy, noise, and visual ugliness (Hirsch, 1977). Judgments differ about the extent to which the quantitative rise in the American standard of living has been offset by qualitative deterioration. Few would dispute, however, that the qualitative deterioration has been significant. Yet, on balance, the evidence is utterly convincing that the past thirty years have seen a major upward trend in the American standard of living—even when both quantitative and qualitative factors are considered.

The Physical Environment. The growth of production and the rise in the American standard of living has, of course, exerted severe pressure on the environment. (See Appendix Tables A11, A12, A13.) It has increased the use of energy, water, and solid materials. And it has increased the amount of waste to be disposed of in the air, in the water, and on the land. Wanton depletion of natural resources and pollution of the environment have a long history in America as the decimated forests, the exhausted mines, the eroded farms, and the grimy cities of the nineteenth and early twentieth centuries testify. Interest in conservation and environmental protection are by no means new to America, but in the past decade or two, the need has become more urgent, the interest has become more intense, and the effort has been redoubled. Tables A11, A12, and A13 present data on trends relative to resource use and the control and abatement of pollution.

The per capita use of energy in the United States grew prodigiously from 1950 to 1970 (though at a somewhat slower rate than world consumption). Since 1970, the U.S. rate of growth has slowed (Table A11). Efforts to conserve energy during the past decade—efforts such as improving the efficiency of generators and motors, reducing speed of motor vehicles, and, above all, allowing the price of energy to rise—have slowed the annual increase in energy use and eventually may reverse the historic upward trend. Nevertheless, the United States still consumes nearly a third of the world's energy and the percentage of U.S. energy needs met by domestic production has been steadily declining. The generation of electricity by nuclear power has grown at a rapid rate from a very small base, but still provides only a minute fraction of America's energy.

The use of water has been erratic depending on the supply, but the trend has been strongly upward. For example, the per capita use of ground water (daily average) has steadily and rapidly increased from 230 gallons in 1950 to 384 gallons in 1975. There is little evidence of conservation of this valuable resource—though evidence abounds that water tables are falling disastrously. The quantity of materials used per capita, as measured by domestic intercity freight traffic or by solid waste disposal, has continued to increase over the period 1950 to 1979, but has shown some signs of leveling off since 1970.

The various indexes of resource use and conservation suggest that the rates of increase have possibly been slowing down. But they also suggest that efforts at conservation have not yet achieved substantial results. Conservation seems to be a case of running faster just to stay even.

The data on pollution are a bit more encouraging (Table A12). Some progress has been achieved in the abatement of air and water pollution, and the production of synthetic organic pesticides has been declining. At the same time, however, the steady accumulation of radioactive wastes presents a difficult and worrisome problem. The nation has been spending large and increasing sums of money for the abatement and control of pollution (Table A13). Substantial sums have been spent by government and even more by private business and individuals. However, with the onset of rapid inflation, the amount of these expenditures in constant dollars has ceased to grow and may even be declining. The conclusion from the fragmentary data available is that progress toward both resource conservation and pollution abatement has been sluggish. Even though the issues have been widely discussed, and large sums of money have been expended, the nation has not been able (or has not had the will) to achieve major progress. But the pell-mell trend toward disaster has probably been slowed if not reversed. The nation has been wrestling with a moral choice between the goal of economic growth and the goal of protecting, preserving, and improving the environment. So far, the weight of public opinion has leaned toward economic growth. The widespread belief and hope is that through "technology" conventional economic growth can be maintained while conserving resources and improving the environment. But this hope will ultimately prove to be vain.

Conditions of Work. Data on this subject are fairly sparse. (See Appendix Table A14.) Studies of workers' attitudes indicate that the great majority express satisfaction with their jobs. The number of workers in manufacturing who were let go by their employers (separations) has declined and the number of workers who quit has increased. These figures doubtless reflect changes in the state of the labor market from time to time, but they also suggest that the economic power of the workers has not deteriorated. The rate of deaths and injuries from industrial accidents has declined substantially. Labor union membership has fallen off relative to the numbers of the nonagricultural wage and salary workers. This decline probably reflects the reduction in the proportion of workers in blue-collar occupations. The trend in the number of strikes has been upward, but the trend in percentage of workers involved has been downward. Finally, average weekly hours of work have fallen moderately. All of these data, taken together, strongly suggest that the conditions of work did not deteriorate and probably improved considerably.

The Distribution of Income. Substantial progress toward equality in the distribution of income received by families has occurred over the past three decades. (See Appendix Tables A15 and A16.) Most of the change took place, however, between 1950 and 1970 when welfare, Social Security, and other social programs were expanding rapidly and their benefits were increasing. Since 1970, under conditions of relatively stable welfare programs, rapid inflation, increasing interest rates, and economic instability, the trend toward greater equality has leveled off and some backsliding has occurred. Nevertheless, when family incomes are compared with the official poverty level, it becomes evident that great progress toward eliminating poverty was made in the years prior to 1970 and that some progress has continued since 1970. The percentage of families judged to be "poor" in 1978 was half that in 1960.

Another way of looking at change in the distribution of income is to observe its division among the several major sources (Table A16). There has been a substantial increase in the proportion received as compensation of employees—a large part of it in the form of wage supplements—and a corresponding decrease in the proportion received from sources related to securities and other property. The trends among these sources related to property were, however, mixed. Proprietors' income as a percentage of the total fell precipitously, but income from interest increased sharply, reflecting the dramatic rise both in debt and in interest rates.

Altogether, the evidence seems clear that the nation achieved considerable progress toward equality of family income from 1950 to 1970 and on the whole held that progress during the 1970s despite the economic turmoil of that decade.

Inflation. The phenomenon of inflation is so conspicuous and so detrimental to the nation that no extended discussion of it is called for. (See Appendix Table A17.) The three major price indexes show that the general price level has about trebled over the past thirty years. To explain and interpret inflation, one should recognize that it is a worldwide condition and that the rate has been relatively less in the United States than in most (but not all) countries. Moreover, some of what we call inflation is due to costs that are socially imposed by government or by social pressure, for example, costs connected with required abatement of pollution, health and safety regulations, extended vacations and coffee breaks, severance pay, and hundreds of other comparable items (Bowen, 1980b, chap. 4; Denison, 1978). Also, some of the inflation is due to the increases in energy costs, mortgage interest rates, and other special factors. Many explanations for the remaining hard-core inflation are given. Most of it, however, is due to the combined effort of the various actors in the economy to extract more products and services from the economy than it is capable of delivering. The question of causation will be considered further in Chapter Four.

Social Conditions

Social Welfare. The term *social welfare* has many meanings. (See Appendix Tables A18 and A19.) In the present context, it refers to activities of the society intended to promote the economic security, health, enlightenment, and general well-being of the population. It includes income maintenance (public assistance, Social Security, veterans' benefits, and so on), health services (pharmaceuticals and the services of hospitals and physicians, for example), and education in all its forms. These activities are financed partly by private organizations and individuals and partly by federal, state, and local government. The basic trends in aggregate expenditures of American society for social welfare over the past thirty years have been strongly upward, indicating a major effort to improve the lot of Americans. As a percentage of the GNP, these expenditures have been doubled since 1950. When expressed in constant dollars per capita, they have increased more than fourfold. Public expenditures for social welfare as a percentage of the total budget of government have nearly doubled. Indeed, these trends have been so strong that the period since World War II might aptly be labeled the era of social welfare.

There is, of course, considerable controversy over the value of these expenditures. Many critics hold that they have been wasteful by giving rise to abuse and fraud or weakening incentives for work and saving. Some go so far as to claim that they have eroded the "moral fibre" of the nation. On the other hand, other observers argue that they have reduced poverty, enhanced personal security, improved health, opened up opportunity, increased justice, and contributed to human dignity. I prefer the second interpretation, though I do not defend the programs in every detail. From the data in Table A18, I conclude that, in the decades since World War II, the nation became committed as never before to human well-being and justice and to the conservation and development of its human resources.

This achievement represents a new concern for social equality and a growing sensitivity to the evils of discrimination based on sex, race, age, religion, handicap, and physical appearance. The result has been substantial progress toward fairness and mutual respect among people. Perfect equality has not been attained—far from it—and discrimination continues to lurk in the shadows of American society, but enormous and heartening progress has been made.

America has a tradition of philanthropy, part of it in the form of internal private gifts for education, the arts, health, welfare, and other purposes and part of it in the form of federal aid to foreign nations. Over the period since 1960, private philanthropy nearly doubled in constant dollars and held steady as a percentage of the GNP (Table A19). An estimated 37 million persons were engaged in volunteer service for philanthropic causes in 1975. Federal aid to foreign nations, however, when measured in constant dollars, declined steadily since 1950. In 1979 the amount was only half what it had been in 1950. The decline was even more pronounced when foreign aid is measured as a percentage of the GNP. Clearly, the beneficiaries of philanthropy—especially the foreign beneficiaries—did not share in America's rising prosperity.

The Family. Perhaps no institution has experienced more fundamental change over the past thirty years than the family. (See Appendix Table A20.) Some observers—perhaps with good cause—refer to what has been happening as the "breakdown" of the family.

Perhaps a more charitable interpretation would be to regard it as a transitional stage of adjustment to such interrelated factors as changing technologies in the home and in the workplace, new birth control methods, unprecedented levels of income, increased personal freedom, new styles of life, and new mores. In reviewing the data pertaining to the family one finds that a marked change in the direction of major trends occurred during the 1960s. Therefore, in commenting on the family I shall concentrate on changes since 1965.

First, note that the society has not rejected marriage. The great majority of people marry at some time, and at any given time about two thirds of the adult population over the age of eighteen are married (Table A20). But the trend in the percentage married and in the percentage of families with two spouses present has been downward. Correspondingly, the trend in percentage of families with only one spouse present has been sharply upward. Nearly 12 million children live in one-parent families. The marriage rate among young women has also been going down, indicating that they are postponing marriage to later ages. The divorce rate is sharply upward to the point that about half of all first marriages end in divorce. The birthrate and the average size of families have been declining, but the premarital pregnancy rate and birthrate (mostly involving teenage girls) has been sharply upward. In 1979, about 1 million teenage girls became pregnant and 600 thousand of them gave birth. The chances of a girl of fourteen becoming pregnant before she turns nineteen were 40 percent. Meanwhile, the abortion rate for women of all ages has also risen rapidly. And the participation of married women in the labor force has been rising dramatically until today about half of all married women (with husbands present) are in the labor force.

There are sharp differences of opinion about the acceptability of current trends relating to the family. Clearly, they signify fundamental and continuing changes in a major social institution. Few would argue, I think, that the nation has reached a satisfactory equilibrium in which the interests and claims of the several parties— fathers, mothers, children, and society—are nicely balanced. It is possible, perhaps likely, that the nation is headed toward multiple solutions such that there will no longer be one predominant form of the family, but many kinds of families (or associations too temporary to be called families) suited to different personalities and varied circumstances. Meanwhile, the nation has almost certainly been losing ground in those aspects of the family related to the rearing of children. Moreover, the current afflictions of the family reflect part of a general shift in values in which personal freedom and self-indulgence are esteemed more highly than responsibility toward other people, including especially children, who make up the traditional family.

Longevity and Health. The trend of longevity since 1950 has been clearly upward. (See Appendix Tables A21 and A22.) Life expectancy has increased by five years, an almost incredible gain. During the same period, the overall death rate declined steadily and the infant mortality rate fell spectacularly. The suicide rate, however, increased slowly but steadily, beginning in 1955. Suicides are too few to add much to the overall death rate, but changes in the suicide rate may reflect shifts in the morale of the population. (Even after the increase from 1955 to 1975, suicide rates were below the historic rates prevailing in the late 1920s and the 1930s.)

The available indicators of trends in health and illness among the living population are ambiguous. They are difficult to interpret because it is hard to separate changes in the incidence of illness from changes in the disposition to report illness, to consult physicians, to enter hospitals, and to take time off from work or school because of illness. As a recent review of the subject concluded (Wilson, Feldman, and Kovar, 1978, p. 148), "Recent trends in illness and disability levels have been . . . difficult to identify. . . . The effects of changes in the provisions of social insurance and changes in accessibility to medical care are practically indistinguishable from changes in the more physiological aspects of health status."

Some statistics relating to health and illness are shown in Appendix Tables A21 and A22. One reasonably objective indicator of health is the height and weight of young persons. Both have increased substantially since 1960. The trends in the incidence of chronic and acute conditions and in disability days have been mixed. These trends probably declined until about 1970 and increased thereafter. Whether this pattern was due to actual changes in health or to changes in subjective attitudes and behavior patterns is uncertain. Finally, substantial changes have occurred since 1950 in the incidence of various specific diseases. For most of these diseases, the numbers have decreased, but for several of them the numbers have increased, among them, salmonellosis, gonorrhea, hepatitis, streptococcal sore throat, and tick-borne typhus (Rocky Mountain spotted fever). What is not shown in this table is the incidence of disorders involving cancer, stroke, and heart disease. There is considerable evidence that recovery rates from these diseases have been rising and the death rates falling.

The conclusions from the data on health are that the longevity of the American people has increased substantially, their height and weight has been increasing, and the state of their health, as conventionally defined, has been improving. In a recent report (*Los Angeles Times*, December 6, 1980, p. I-3), the Surgeon General of the United States declared that "the health of the American people has never been better."

Drug Addiction and Alcoholism. Health in general may have been improving, but in two respects, namely drug addiction and alcoholism, the well-being of the American people has been deteriorating. Historical statistics on the use of drugs and alcohol are scarce and difficult to interpret, but the number of persons involved has grown explosively in recent decades.

"Reported narcotic addict/abusers" in 1973 numbered about 100 thousand (U.S. Bureau of the Census, *Statistical Abstract of the United States*, 1975, p. 89). However, this figure included only those persons known to law enforcement agencies and voluntarily reported to the Drug Enforcement Administration and did not begin to count all addicts and abusers, let alone users. Drug abuse is a special problem of youth. Most users are either young people or persons who began drug use when they were young. Of the 100 thousand "addict/abusers" reported, 70 percent were thirty years old or under.

In a 1970 study of alcoholism, it was estimated that 5.4 million persons were alcoholics defined as "one who is unable consistently to choose whether he shall drink or not, and who, if he drinks, is unable consistently to choose whether he shall stop or not" (U.S. Bureau of the Census; *Statistical Abstract*, 1975, p. 88). The rate of alcoholism was about 4 percent of the adult population.

Alcohol is a factor in 10 percent of all deaths in the United States (National Institute of Alcohol Abuse and Alcoholism). The heavy incidence occurs in adult life, but use of alcohol often begins in the teens. In a recent study, the Research Triangle Institute reported that most American teenagers drink alcoholic beverages and that one third of the nation's high school students are "problem drinkers" (*New York Times*, March 20, 1981).

Data on high school seniors reveal the emergence of drug and alcohol problems during youth. These data are derived from an authoritative nationwide study conducted by the Survey Research Center of the University of Michigan (Johnston, Bachman, and O'Malley, 1980). According to this study, about 60 percent of high school seniors report that they had used marijuana or hashish at some time in the past and 26 percent that they had used them in the past thirty days; 10 percent or more had at some time used other drugs such as LSD, cocaine, and amphetamines, and 2 to 10 percent had used one or more of these drugs in the past thirty days. Many were repeaters, having used the drugs two or more times during the past thirty days. Almost all the high school seniors had imbibed alcoholic beverages at some time. Over 72 percent of them reported that they had used alcoholic beverages within the past month, and 40 percent said that they had taken five or more drinks in a row within the past two weeks. Note that these figures pertain only to high school seniors and omit the high school dropouts among whom the use of drugs and alcohol are almost certainly greater than among those about to graduate from high school.

Crime. The trend of crime in the United States, like the state of health, is not easy to trace. (See Appendix Tables A23 and A24.) There can be no doubt, however, that crime has increased statistically during the past thirty years. Almost every indicator shows a vast and disturbing growth of criminal activity. The statistics, however, probably overstate the increase for several reasons: (1) the trend of crime had been generally downward from 1933 to 1960, and so subsequent increases, which were concentrated in the years 1960 to 1975, represented growth from an unusually low base; (2) the reporting of crimes probably increased as the population became more integrated and confidence in the police became more widespread; (3) recordkeeping and statistical reporting by the police probably improved; and (4) since a large fraction of all crime is committed by youthful offenders, the sudden growth in the youthful cohorts following the postwar baby boom produced more people in the prime criminal ages. For all these reasons, the statistics should not be taken at face value, yet, most informed observers believe that even after allowance for several factors, true crime rates did increase substantially, especially during the period from 1960 to 1975. Of special interest to educators is that crime rates are extremely high among persons in the age group from eleven to twenty-four—the age group for which educators at the secondary and higher level are explicitly responsible.

Communications, Education, Arts, and Science

Communications. Almost every aspect of communications has undergone explosive growth over the past thirty years. (See Appendix Table A25.) The one important exception is the number and circulation of newspapers, but even these have expanded in the sense that the consumption of newsprint per capita has increased substantially. The nation is literally bombarded with information and entertainment. The most dramatic change has been the growth of television, which has expanded from almost nothing to near saturation of the society. The expansion of popular music in recordings and live performances and of hard-core pornography has been startling. Perhaps the most comprehensive indicator of the explosion of communications is total expenditures for advertising. Total advertising outlays have nearly doubled even when these figures are expressed per capita and in constant dollars. Thus, the average person in the United States today is assailed by nearly twice as much advertising as he or she might have received in 1950, only thirty years ago, and the overall amount of mass communications of all kinds has probably increased equivalently. In interpreting this growth, remember that in 1950 the average American was already receiving enormous amounts of information and persuasion, especially through the radio.

People differ in their judgments about the effects of the increase of communications. On the one hand, some of the easily available information from the mass media is educative in a positive sense. People are in touch with events and ideas from all over the world. In some respects, it reinforces the efforts of the traditional educational institutions, such as schools, colleges, churches, libraries, museums, musical organizations, and others. Moreover, the mass media provide an enormous amount of pleasure and recreation for their audiences—though often of a passive and stupefying sort. On the other hand, the information disseminated by the mass media comes overwhelmingly from sources that are anything but disinterested—sources whose main concern is not improving minds, communicating sound values, or enriching the culture. Rather, they are bent on *selling*—selling cigarettes, cereal, cars, or cosmetics. They are not above whatever level of false values, vulgarity, or sensationalism is necessary to make the sale. They incessantly preach the gospel of material gratification. To an alarming degree, the mass media work directly and powerfully at cross-purposes to the school, the college, the church, and the other traditional educational agencies. Even David Ogilvy, a leading producer of advertisements who now lives in France, recently said in an interview, "When I come back, I see things through newer eyes. I've been watching the television and I'm really appalled at the amount of advertising. It seems to me to project a culture which is becoming terribly materialistic. The sound of selling is the dirge of our time" (*Los Angeles Times,* April 2, 1981, p. IV-1).

Voting. Though communications in general have been on the increase, a singularly important form of communication, namely, participation of the American people in elections, has been declining steadily for many years (Table A26). For example, in the 1980 national election, only 53 percent of the voting age population actually went to the polls. President Reagan won what is often called a "landslide" victory or a "mandate" with only a little more than 25 percent of those eligible to vote casting their ballots for him. It is highly doubtful that the minority who go to the polls are representative of the total population. The proportion of the people who consider themselves members of a political party also has been declining over many years.

Education. The progress of education was described in Chapters One and Two and will not be repeated here. Suffice it to say that an immense application of money and effort has been devoted to the task of raising the educational attainments of the American people (Appendix Tables A27, A28, and A29). Given the known effects of education on the personal development of individuals and on the advancement of society, this effort surely has not been in vain. However, the present and prospective educational attainments of the American people are still far short of their potentialities.

The Fine Arts. The arts in America have been booming. (See Appendix Table A30.) In the case of the performing arts, the number of new works composed, the number of performances, and the size of audiences have all been increasing at an astonishing rate. The graphic and plastic arts have also been flourishing. Museums of all kinds are experiencing unprecedented public interest and attendance. To document this, one has only to witness the long lines of people crowding into leading museums everywhere. This growing interest in the arts is reflected also in the rapid extension of federal aid to the arts and humanities. All these facts say nothing about the quality of the artistic life of America. However, it is safe to assert that the nation has made qualitative as well as quantitative progress over recent decades.

Science and Technology. The nation has enjoyed remarkable growth in scientific activity and technological development during the past thirty years. (See Appendix Table A31.) The rate of growth from 1950 to 1970 was especially rapid; after 1970, there was some leveling off, but no perceptible decline. Available statistics do not address the question of quality or fruitfulness of scientific and technological activity. Some informed observers express the opinion that the quality may have declined a bit. However, the stunning successes of American space explorations, the spectacular achievements in biology and medicine, American leadership in computer technology, the successes in military applications of science, and the Nobel Prize scoreboard all suggest that American science and technology are by no means laggard. However, investments in science and technology, like all other investments, are subject to diminishing returns. Pushing out the frontiers of science and technology becomes increasingly costly and given increments of investment yield successively smaller returns.

Quality of Life

So far, my review of the progress of the nation over the past thirty years has emphasized trends that could be described largely by means of quantitative data. There are other important trends which, though essentially qualitative and not easily measured, must not be ignored. Indeed it is these that future historians of the era will undoubtedly judge to be the most fundamental and significant developments of the past generation.

Perhaps the most momentous change of the past thirty years has been the increasing concern for submerged groups of the population. This concern has been expressed in increasingly tolerant attitudes toward these groups and in legislation outlawing various types of adverse discrimination against them.

Though the gains are constantly vulnerable to erosion, substantial progress—social, economic, political, and attitudinal—has been achieved by the submerged groups. For example, much of the discrimination against Jews has disappeared, and the historic prejudice toward Roman Catholics has largely subsided. In the case of the Catholics, the influence of Pope John XXIII and the election of John Kennedy to the presidency were notable factors in the attitudinal change. At the same time, various European ethnic groups such as the Italians and the Poles have on the whole achieved social status virtually equal to that of descendants of northern European immigrants. The position of Orientals has also risen markedly. In many ways, the status of women has improved, although the sudden entry of millions of them into the labor force has tended to slow advancement in their rate of compensation. The position of handicapped persons, individuals of atypical physical appearance, homosexuals, and the elderly has also risen. The case of the blacks and Hispanics is somewhat different. The problem of bringing them into the mainstream of American life has been extraordinarily difficult because of their large numbers and because of a deeply ingrained legacy of prejudice and overt suppression. Nevertheless, many members of both groups are gaining in education, political influence, income, and status. Thousands—perhaps millions—are entering the American middle and upper classes. Generally, in the past several decades the various marks of discrimination have been widely challenged and discredited.

The significant progress is partially documented in Appendix Table A32, which shows relative gains on the part of minorities with respect to education, income, life expectancy, voter registration, and election to public office. However, relative rates of unemployment for minorities have increased and relative earnings for women have fallen. As all authentic appraisals of the situation agree, full equality is still only a distant ideal.* The expansion of human rights during the postwar period was not an isolated event in American history but an incident in a long succession of forward thrusts in the fulfillment of democratic ideals. As Max Lerner (1976, pp. 88–89) has suggested:

> One could rewrite the history of America in the past two hundred years as a succession of efforts to come ever closer to a society of equal access, from the Jeffersonian and Jacksonian Revolutions through the Civil War, the Populist movement of the 1880s and 1890s, the intellectual renaissance of the turn of the century, the New Nationalism of Theodore Roosevelt, the New Freedom of Wilson, the New Deal and the Fair Deal of Franklin Roosevelt and Harry Truman, the New Frontier and the Great Society of John Kennedy and Lyndon Johnson. I have used the political slogans, both for brevity and to express the fact that political-social reform movements get what strength they possess from their congruence with both the discontents and the passionate strivings of the people themselves.

Closely related to the rise of submerged groups has been a remarkable expansion of personal freedom among people of all classes. The range of socially tolerable behavior has been greatly extended. Freedom of choice has been widened with respect to diet, clothing, housing, work, leisure pursuits, sexual mores, marriage and divorce, child care, use of alcohol and drugs, and all the other aspects of behavior that are called collectively "lifestyle." Traditional demands for formality have been relaxed and the expression of individuality encouraged. Just as prejudice toward the submerged groups has been lessened, so prejudice toward persons who deviate from traditional norms of conduct has been reduced—sometimes to the extent that conventional persons become victims of prejudice.

*See, for example, President's Commission for a National Agenda for the Eighties (1980a, pp. 7–24).

At the same time, the rights (including powers, privileges, and immunities) of individuals have been strengthened. The new emphasis on rights has taken many forms. Of special importance has been a marked increase in the influence of rank-and-file individuals in the conduct of the body politic, big business, universities, and other organizations. Some of the gains in influence have come about through collective bargaining, some through belligerent protests as in the case of "marches" on city hall or student riots, and some from the courts as they have insisted on due process in many organizational decisions affecting individuals. Meanwhile, citizens, employees, and rank-and-file members of organizations have learned effective techniques of communicating and enforcing their demands. In particular, interest groups have gained expertise in pulling the levers that bring power to bear on political and organizational decision making. Still another development affecting the quality of life has been the increasing attention of government—especially the federal government—to protecting the safety and health of workers and consumers.

Taken together, the rise of the submerged groups, the widening of personal freedom, the strengthening of human rights, and the protection of workers and consumers have brought about far-reaching—almost revolutionary—changes in the American way of life. Controversy has continually swirled around these developments and still goes on. From time to time there have been reversals of these trends—even including backlash from those whose relative economic or social position may have been threatened or diminished. Yet, on balance, equality, freedom, and rights have been extended to millions of people. By the 1980s, these changes had worked their way irreversibly into American life—though their influence may fluctuate from time to time with changing political currents.

Over and against the expansion of equality, freedom, rights, and protections are some qualitative trends that are more difficult to evaluate. Many observers believe that large numbers of people today, as compared with their forebears, have become preoccupied with their own interests, pleasures, and comforts, and are inclined to shirk their responsibilities as citizens, family members, and workers. Words such as *materialism, self-indulgence, hedonism, narcissism,* and *privatism* are used to describe these people. They are said to be mainly interested in carefree lives of consumption, leisure, and excitement, to have lost the work ethic, and to lack the guidance of a valid system of ultimate beliefs and values. As a result, it is said that their citizenship is based on narrow self-interest, their family responsibilities are neglected, and they lack a sense of vocation in their work. Such generalizations are problematic. Obviously they do not apply to all or even most members of the present population. Moreover, memories are imperfect as to the values and inclinations of people of other eras. For example, the people of the Edwardian era, of the roaring 1920s, or of the silent generation of the 1950s may have been as keen on material gratification as the present generation, though perhaps with greater emphasis on invidious consumption designed for keeping up or getting ahead of one's neighbors. It is hard to plot such moral trends accurately.

Another profoundly important contemporary social movement tends to offset or counteract the alleged rise of hedonism: the rapid growth in numbers of people who have taken up religious belief and practice of the evangelical, charismatic, or Oriental varieties. However, the extent of this involvement is disputed. Some polls have suggested that as much as 25 to 30 percent of the population is interested or active in new religious movements (Broder, 1981). Martin (1981) estimates that only about 9 million households, or about 12 percent of all households, are involved in such movements, and that the number is probably declining; this estimate is probably the more reliable one.

The revival of religious interest is not wholly contrary to hedonistic tendencies in that some of the newer varieties of religion are focused on the self (peace of mind or personal salvation) without much emphasis on social responsibility. Some are characterized by unlovely bigotry and some by tendencies to confuse quite earthly political opinions with the word of God. Nevertheless, the religious revival in some of its forms represents a trend that runs counter to hedonistic tendencies. It may represent a search for a sense of well-being beyond economic abundance and material gratification. Thus, in the present fluid situation, it is too soon to declare that hedonism occupies a lasting or dominant influence in contemporary American life. As Peter Clecak (in press) has observed: "During the sixties and seventies, . . . Americans engaged in a search for ful-fillment, an open-ended quest for distinctive syntheses of personal salvation and shares of social justice. Tens of millions of citizens within overlapping social categories sought—and in varying degrees discovered—paths to fuller definitions and expressions of themselves as individuals and as participants in one or more rela-tively small communities. This seems to me the most striking—and hopeful—fact about American culture in these years."

Finally, no discussion of the quality of life in America would be complete without reference to vast changes during the past thirty years in the global environment of the nation. The speed and ease of international communication and travel have increased greatly and contacts among peoples of the earth have multiplied. The sheer bulk of international commerce has grown tremendously. Enormous efforts have been expended on the international transmission of knowledge, culture, and technology and on assistance to the peoples of less-developed countries. Multinational corporations and public and private agencies for international cooperation have mush-roomed. In these ways, the world has become more cosmopolitan, more interdependent, and more integrated. The trend toward world unity has perhaps been accentuated by the space explorations of the past several decades. These have given peoples everywhere a sense of a common destiny as occupants of a tiny, beautiful, fragile, and productive planet.

Unfortunately, these integrative influences have been more than matched by powerful and insidious divisive forces. The influ-ences that divide the peoples of the earth reflect in part differences in wealth and income and differences in ethnic origin, language, reli-gion, national tradition, and political ideology. These differences seem to have become more intense and more inflammatory in recent decades. They have led to constant turmoil and to frequent wars, cold wars, and threats of war. In an age of nuclear and other sophis-ticated armaments, these influences could bring on the ultimate disaster of nuclear holocaust. At the least, they impel the nations to devote a disproportionate and increasing amount of their resources to military purposes.

Yet, despite the turmoil, the actual wars since 1950 have all been local in scope, of limited duration, and fought with nonnuclear weapons. Nothing of the scale of World War I and II has occurred, and since Hiroshima and Nagasaki the world has been spared catastrophic nuclear detonations.

Conclusions

By the standards commonly used in measuring the program of a nation, the data and arguments in this chapter have described an era of remarkable economic and social progress. The facts seem to belie the common beliefs that the American people are economically worse off than they were thirty years ago, that federal spending has been out of control and is the chief cause of inflation, or that the social programs of the past several decades have failed (see Pifer, 1981). Despite serious problems and setbacks (the problem of war being the most serious), the past thirty years would surely rank as one of the more creative times in American history. Consider these achievements over the period from 1950 to 1980:

- The population has grown but the rate of growth has declined and the number of people should level off in the twenty-first century. The Malthusian spectre may have been overcome—at least in the United States.
- The proportion of the population in the older age groups has increased, but the proportion in the younger age groups has declined. As a result of these counteracting tendencies, the dependency ratio, that is, the ratio of persons above or below the normal working age to those of working age, has stabilized.
- Production per capita (after adjustment for inflation) has almost doubled. The United States is the world's largest national economy, producing about 20 percent of the world's output and conducting over 10 percent of the world's trade.
- The number of new jobs has increased by nearly 40 million or by 64 percent. Record numbers of women and young people have been successfully inducted into the labor force.
- Vast changes have occurred in the structure of the economy: relatively more production of services and less of goods, relatively more employment in white-collar jobs and less in blue-collar jobs.

- The proportion of the economy devoted to government, as measured by goods and services purchased, has declined. However, with the increase in transfer payment, mostly designed to overcome poverty and to increase human well-being, government expenditures as a percentage of the GNP have increased moderately.
- The standard of living of the American people, after correction for inflation, has doubled.
- Important beginnings have been made in the conservation of natural resources and the protection of the environment.
- Hours of labor have declined moderately, and job satisfaction has been consistently at a high level, although it has not risen.
- The distribution of income has become significantly more equitable, and the incidence of poverty has declined sharply.
- Longevity has been extended by five years, and on the average, health has been improved.
- Public and private expenditures for social welfare (health, income maintenance, education, and other welfare services) have grown enormously as the nation has become more sensitive to the preservation and improvement of human resources.
- Communications, the arts, science, and technology have all flourished.
- The nation has made a quantum leap forward in equality for various minority groups and—in some respects—for women. In addition, human freedom has been expanded, human rights extended, and workers and consumers protected from injury and noxious products.

These are, on the whole, substantial gains and should arouse second thoughts among those who see the state of America darkly and view the future with apprehension. The rate of improvement may not have been equal to the potential or in some respects equal to the progress of a few other nations. But with allowance for the maturity of the American economy and for the already high levels of economic and social attainment in America in the base year of 1950, the performance of American society has been impressive.

Significantly, scarcely any item in the long list of achievements would have been attainable without the *widening and deep-*

ening of higher education that occurred in the postwar period. The overall record is, among other things, a testimonial to the productive achievements of the academic community.

Yet there is indeed a darker side of the postwar era. There have been and continue to be obvious and grievous problems, most of which have been alluded to in our survey of the state of the nation. As Alan Pifer (1981) has pointed out, however, "The remaining problems signify not that the social programs have failed but that the agenda of social reform is far from finished." It is to this agenda that we turn in the next chapter.

Problems Facing the Nation   4   ✤✤✤✤

"A culture's educational ideals for its citizens, and the de facto ideals that its educational institutions carry, are the products of a vision of the good society, of what ought to be . . . . Educational institutions are the bearers of our value-laden social wills."

—Martin Kaplan (1980, pp. 5–6)

Among the economic and social trends presented in the last chapter were certain adverse developments that call for further consideration. It is the unsolved problems rather than the successes that define the agenda of the nation. These problems are well known; their identity will surprise no one. Indeed, since both politicians and the media tend to dwell on adversity more than success, the problems of the nation are well advertised. There is little dispute about their identity though much disagreement about priorities and solutions. There are ten of these problems:

1. Economic problems:
    (a)   inflation
    (b)   unemployment
    (c)   environmental deterioration and resource depletion
2. Social problems:
    (a)   crime
    (b)   drug abuse and alcoholism
3. Educational problems:
    (a)   the family
    (b)   school and neighborhood

(c)   mass media
4. Political problems:
   (a)   pressure-group democracy
   (b)   war and the threat of war

These ten widely recognized national problems underlie the true agenda of the nation. At first glance, they seem to cover a wide range, to have little in common, and to call for quite varied solutions. Yet, on closer inspection, many of them reveal two distinctive features in common. First, most are rooted in the failure of people— individually, as groups, or as a society—to act responsibly on the basis of acknowledged *values*. Second, many of these problems fall with special severity on *youth*. From these two features it follows that higher education has an important—perhaps critical—role in the amelioration of most of these problems. Higher education, potentially at least, is a powerful instrument for transmitting values and for facilitating the personal growth and development of youth. Of course, higher education is not solely responsible for the transmittal of values or for the redemption of youth. It shares these responsibilities with other institutions. In achieving the agenda of the nation, many things must be done by many agencies. Yet higher education has an indispensable role, as I shall testify in later chapters. In this chapter, I shall comment briefly on each of the ten problems from the point of view of their relationship to *values* and to *youth*.

Economic Problems

Inflation. The nation has been confronted with inflation during most of the postwar period. Until about 1965, the price increases were gradual, averaging 1 or 2 percent a year. After that year they continued at an accelerating rate and during much of the 1970s and early 1980s ranged from 6 to 11 percent a year.

Many explanations of inflation are offered. Fundamentally, however, it is due to the effort to extract from the economy more goods and services than the economy is capable of delivering. This happens when business tries to get higher prices, workers press for higher wages, consumers try to live beyond their means, government tries to obtain more resources for waging war or advancing social development, and government supplies the money to support all these efforts. Once inflation takes hold, it becomes embedded in the expectations of the economic actors in ways that perpetuate and accentuate it. By drastically curtailing the supply of money, it can be stopped; technically, governments are capable of this. But such monetary curtailment is risky in that it may precipitate depression, which is even worse than inflation.

Inflation, in short, is fundamentally a product of human acquisitiveness and lack of concern for the public interest. It can be overcome without disastrous depression only when people are willing, individually and collectively, to make sacrifices in favor of the long-term general good. Walter Heller (1980b) described the phenomenon in this way:

> Inflation grows out of our social commitment to a high-employment, low-misery society—in a word, a humane society. . . . By eliminating the cruel "discipline" of depression, by reducing the pain and misery of unemployment, by raising aspirations and expectations, we have made not just our economy but our society inflation prone. The powerful income claims of strongly organized producer groups—large businesses, labor unions, farm groups—simply exceed the total size of the economic pie. . . . Lacking a reliable mechanism to reconcile these conflicting claims, we have accumulated them by inflation. . . . Or to strip the problem down to its essence, we all want more than there is. That is the inflationary devil within us. In this sense, then, the roots of inflation lie deep in our social structure, in our psyche, in our institutions, and in our democratic ethic.

Unemployment. A nagging problem of American society is the inability to employ all the persons who are seeking work. The trend of unemployment has been slowly moving upward over the past thirty years. Unemployment, however, is concentrated especially among young people, particularly those with limited education and those from minority groups. The unemployment rate for workers of ages sixteen to nineteen is about 16 percent and for those of ages twenty to twenty-four about 10 percent whereas the corresponding percentage for males in the prime working ages of twenty-five to sixty-five is around 3 percent (see Table A5). To look at youth unemployment in terms of numbers of persons, of the 6 million of all ages who were unemployed in 1978, a full quarter, or 1.5 million, were below the age of twenty. These figures do not reflect the full gravity of the situation, however, because many young people are discouraged from trying to find work and simply drop out of the labor force. The figures in Table 4 show the full extent to which youth are not working—whether or not they are technically unemployed.

It is understandable that unskilled and inexperienced young people would have more difficulty finding jobs than older, more experienced persons. Nevertheless, society has an obvious obligation either to find ways of employing these people in useful work of a kind that would develop skills and good work habits or to provide suitable educational experiences for them.

Environmental Deterioration and Resource Depletion. The nation and the whole world, as well, face the twin environmental problems of pollution in all its many forms and natural resource depletion. These problems have been discussed widely and intensively in the United States, considerable regulatory legislation has been enacted, and large sums have been spent on amelioration by government, private firms, and individuals. Nevertheless, actual progress in pollution abatement and conservation has been slow because it has been overwhelmed by changing technology and rapid economic growth. The efforts to date may have retarded the rate of environmental deterioration but they have fallen far short of stopping it. The energy crisis and the acceleration of inflation have both had the effect of discouraging further efforts.

Table 4. Persons 16 to 19 Years of Age, Not in School, 1978

	Not in Labor Force	In Labor Force but Unemployed	Total
Male	11.4%	14.1%	25.5%
Female	30.5	17.2	47.7

Source: U.S. Bureau of the Census, *Social Indicators III* (1980, p. 359).

The question of what ought to be done about the environment, given the technical possibilities, is a matter of social responsibility. In the short run, the question faced by society is: How much immediate gratification in the form of goods and services for consumption should be sacrificed in order to improve the environment and conserve resources? Such sacrifices would occur when the rate of exploitation of certain natural resources (for example, petroleum or timber) was slowed, when consumption of certain goods was reduced (for example, by rationing or taxation), when efforts were made toward preservation or improvement of natural resources (for example, through maintenance of top soil, reforestation, abatement of water pollution, or air quality improvement), and when regulations were imposed to prevent the fouling of the environment (for example, noise ordinances, bans on aerosol sprays, outlawing of dangerous pesticides, control over disposal of toxic wastes). In the long run, the basic question concerns the proper balancing of the interests of future generations against those of the present generation. The principle involved is that the interests of future generations, even those of the distant future, are as important as the interests of the present generation. Peoples of the future have a legitimate right to inherit a world with resources and natural amenities undiminished from those enjoyed by the present generation. Therefore, it is the responsibility of the present generation to pass on a heritage at least equal to that which it received from earlier generations. The heritage consists, however, not only of the physical environment itself but also the stock of knowledge and technology. Often, improvements in knowledge and technology can offset the effects of deterioration of the environment and of the supply of resources. But even with knowledge and technology taken into account, the present generation is not living up to its responsibility toward the future. So long as the nation continues to choose as its highest value economic growth and ever greater consumption (in a quantitative sense), environmental degradation will worsen.

To reduce demands on natural resources and on the environment, however, it is not necessary to curtail employment or cut drastically the standard of living. It is necessary only to seek *qualitative* improvement in the style of life instead of quantitative increases in the bulk of physical goods consumed. For example, demand could be shifted from trendy fashions and disposable commodities to such items as finely crafted furniture of solid wood, appliances and automobiles of high quality and durability, and durable clothing of styles that do not instantly become obsolete. Similarly, demand could be shifted to services such as education, reading, health improvement, home repair, and arts and crafts that make small demands on the physical environment and on natural resources.

Social Problems

Crime. Crime, dishonesty, and disrespect for law have been increasing over the past several decades. It is hard to avoid the word *disgraceful* to describe the situation. Crime in the United States is heavily concentrated among youthful offenders or among people who begin a life of crime at an early age. The crime rate among persons from fifteen to twenty-four years of age is four times what it is among persons twenty-five and over (Appendix Table A24). An indication that youthful crime is not confined to high school dropouts comes from a nationwide survey of high school seniors (Johnston, Bachman, and O'Malley, 1980, pp. 103, 194). Over 20 percent report that they have been in trouble with the police, 33 percent admit to having stolen something, 32 percent report shoplifting, 24 percent have entered a building where they did not belong, 14 percent have damaged school property, and more than 15 percent have been in serious fights, individually or as gangs. Among the more serious offenses, 3 percent have hit an instructor or supervisor, 10 percent have hurt someone, 3 percent have used a knife or gun "to get something," and 4 percent have taken a car. In appraising these figures, note that they relate only to high school seniors and leave out the much higher crime rate among high school dropouts. The onus rests largely on a society that tolerates conditions in the family, the neighborhood, the labor market, the media, and the educational system that lead young people to criminal activity—either by active encouragement or by default.

But crimes of theft and violence are not the whole of the problem. In addition, dishonesty, corruption, deception, and fraud are found commonly in business and government even among our great corporations and our highest public officials (Clinard and Yeager, 1980).

Drug Abuse and Alcoholism. As indicated in Chapter Three, the use and abuse of drugs and alcohol have increased explosively over the past several decades and currently are severe national problems. They are of special concern because of their heavy incidence among youth. The causes of drug addiction and alcoholism are not well understood, and what should be done to correct them or who is responsible for them is unclear. But the problems exist, and there is a clear social responsibility—perhaps shared by the educational system, the criminal justice system, the health care system, and the social welfare system—to bring about amelioration.

Educational Problems

The Family. The nuclear family of husband, wife, and children is a universal institution. It is found in most societies, often as the exclusive form of the family and sometimes as the primary unit of more complex family systems. The family usually carries on three functions: reproduction, education, and production of goods and services relating to the care and welfare of its members. In western society, the traditional nuclear family has usually involved a lifetime contract between husband and wife in which they agree to live together and care for each other and their children.

In America (and other industrial nations as well) the concept of the family has been eroding. Premarital and extramarital sex relations are common, over one fourth of all babies are born out of wedlock, venereal diseases are on the increase, and prostitution and pornography are rampant. With the help of new methods of contraception and the legalization of abortion, the birth rate has fallen to below the level needed to maintain the population. Indeed, the love of children appears to have declined. Increasing numbers of parents apparently regard children as costly nuisances who get in the way of economic, social, and recreational activities and who depress the family standard of living. Child neglect and child abuse are on the rise. More than half of all married women are employed, and many others are deeply involved in social, recreational, political, and educational activities outside the home. About half of all first marriages end in divorce. Though there are still millions of strong traditional families in America, it is safe to say that the condition of other millions is, in varying degrees, unsatisfactory.

The traditional family was supported by a powerful moral code, which valued children highly, demanded loving care of them, and emphasized responsibility of each member for the integrity of the family group. This moral code—never universally followed—has been losing its authority. Indeed, the traditional concept of marriage and the family appears to be undergoing rapid and far-reaching evolution. It is possible that our society is moving gradually toward some new model of the family or even toward multiple models that would allow choice among several approved contractual relationships and among several alternative arrangements for the care of children. But pending the development of such new socially legitimized arrangements, the deterioration of the traditional family must be regarded as an unfortunate lapse of responsibility that clouds the future of many children and many adults as well.

School and Neighborhood. Since World War II, the nation has devoted vast resources to education at all levels. One result has been a quantum leap in the educational attainment of the American people. As shown in Appendix Table A29 and Chapter Two, the percentage of adults with an eighth-grade education or less has declined steadily from 47 percent in 1950 to 18 percent in 1979, and the percentage who have graduated from college has increased from 6 percent in 1950 to 16 percent in 1979. If the present educational system should be continued indefinitely, just as it existed in 1979, the percentage with only a grade school education would decline to 12 percent of the adult population and those with four-year college degrees would rise to 28 percent. These are notable achievements. However, the meagre evidence on the actual ability of people to perform, as distinguished from the number of school grades they have completed, suggests that a quarter to a third have significant educational disabilities including those that border on illiteracy, and that the number of reasonably well-educated persons is and will probably continue to be, a small minority of the population. The American people are far from being overeducated.

In recent years, there has been widespread dissatisfaction with the public schools, especially the high schools. Part of the complaint has been slackness of academic standards, including inadequate attention to the "basics," excessive preoccupation with nonacademic subjects and with extracurricular activities, and declining scores on standardized tests. Part of the criticism has been directed toward the peer culture in many schools and surrounding neighborhoods. In recent decades, this culture has come to include broken families, drugs, alcoholic beverages, street gangs, vandalism, crime, suicides, graphic violence in movies and television, pornography, and premarital births. To illustrate: Since 1950 the rate of death due to homicide among white males of ages fifteen to twenty-four has increased from 3 to 10 per 100,000 persons, the suicide rate among the same group has increased from 6 to 14, and the out-of-wedlock births for white females of ages fifteen to nineteen has risen from 5 to 14 per 100,000. These conditions, which vary greatly among schools and neighborhoods, are most prevalent in urban areas and in low-income neighborhoods, but are by no means confined to these. It is evident that the conditions in schools and in neighborhoods are closely linked. For a great many young people, the cultural matrix in which their values and their style of life are being formed is almost totally inconsistent with the expectations and ideals of American education.

In describing these conditions, I am not necessarily implying that educators in the public schools are neglectful of their duty. Many are caught up in conditions largely beyond their control that make their work extraordinarily difficult, trying, and even dangerous. These same conditions represent an enormous challenge not only to educators but to the whole society.

Mass Media. The mass media of the United States operate under two momentous conditions: (1) freedom of communications as guaranteed in the Constitution and (2) dependence on advertising for financial support. The first of these conditions gives the media almost unlimited control over content and the second motivates them to operate in ways that will maximize clients' sales. Under these conditions, both the electronic and the printed media constantly batter the minds and emotions of the populace with messages—some blatant and some subtle—that suggest, illustrate, and extol without limit the virtues of the things money will buy. They convey these messages not only through advertisements and commercials but also through the substantive content of the articles and programs accompanying the sales pitches. The overall effect is to encourage—almost enforce—hedonism as a central value of our society.

These conditions are not wholly new. The mass media have for generations enjoyed freedom of the press and have been supported mainly by advertising, and they have been far from conveying consistently noble values. However, in an earlier day, the technologies were relatively less effectual. Today, the modern photographic and electronic media operate at a totally different level of influence. A difference in degree has become a difference in kind.

The media are especially influential in their effect on youth. Not only do they convey the basic message of hedonism and narcissism but, in the process, they portray no end of violence, crime, sex, and gossip about "celebrities" in ways that affect the formation of values and character. The influence of the media overall runs almost exactly counter to the moral influence of education and the other character-forming institutions. The media also occupy immense amounts of youthful time that could better be devoted to play, hobbies, sports, friendships, general reading, and study. As Landau (1980) has written, "the content of these shows—whether educational, trivial, or violence promoting—is less significant than the fact that, in all cases, *children sit and watch them*." The same comment might be applied to adults as well.

The media have the important and legitimate economic function of informing consumers about the availability of goods and services. Moreover, a small section of the media consistently provide fare that caters to broader and deeper values—among these media are some newspapers, certain magazines and books, and a few radio and television stations. And perhaps most media devote some of their space or time to material that is not inconsistent with the goals of education. But the overall impact of the media is overwhelmingly supportive of a way of life in which value is equated with the consumption of goods and services, and the content used in conveying this message is, to an alarming degree incompatible with the kinds of values associated with the family, the church, the schools, and the colleges. Indeed, the media have captured many parents and may have neutralized the family as an independent moral force.

The media—even at their best—tend to be detrimental also because of their tendency to present the world in fragments, with little distinction between the important and unimportant or between the enduring and the fleeting. They lack coherence and organizing principles. Events and ideas are evaluated on the basis of their novelty and their power to attract attention rather than of their importance or fundamental truth.

There are, of course, compelling reasons for keeping the media free of censorship and for making them financially independent of government. But such freedom and independence are tolerable only to the extent that the media and their sponsors conduct their activities responsibly—with moderation and with respect for values beyond those associated with ever-expanding consumption. As Leo Strauss declared (1965, p. 96), "liberal education consists in learning to listen to still and small voices and therefore in becoming deaf to loudspeakers."

Political Problems

Pressure-Group Democracy. Many observers of American politics have noted the increasing activity and influence of special interest groups. The political system has become a kind of vast competitive marketplace in which thousands of interest groups exert relentless pressure for particular and narrow political goals. These groups organize meetings, spread propaganda, lobby, give financial and other support to candidates, oppose unfriendly officials, and in some cases give favors or outright bribes. These special groups have become so ubiquitous that the political fate of the nation tends to become the unplanned resultant of innumerable competing pressures. In the workings of this system, the broad public interest is often ignored, especially when the various groups are unequal in their knowledge of how to pull the political levers, in their powers of persuasion, and in their affluence. Of course, narrow interest groups are not new to American politics. Moreover, in a democratic society, all groups must be free to communicate their needs and demands to government and to press their claims. Yet, as the system has evolved, only rarely—mainly in times of crisis or in times of exceptional leadership—do considerations of the broad social welfare transcend the noisy discord of innumerable special interests. The situation is worsened when candidates and government officials rely on the fleeting information from public opinion polls to set their campaign platforms and to guide their official decisions. There is an unfortunate lack in American politics of a tradition of responsible leadership that brings the broad and long-range public interest into the political arena. This matter will be considered at some length in Chapter Five.

War and the Threat of War. No one who has lived through the twentieth century can be indifferent to the threat of war. In this century, the United States has been engaged in four major wars, and throughout the world many other conflicts have broken out. As I write, four separate wars are being fought in various parts of the world. The concern about war has been greatly intensified by the development and proliferation of nuclear armaments, which threatens the ultimate in death and destruction. The threat of war has also grown more dangerous because the peoples of the world have become increasingly zealous to preserve their unique religions, languages, and cultural identities. Sensitivities are easily aroused and the risk of conflict has therefore been increased. The recent resumption in the United States of the cold war mentality and of an arms buildup are disturbing trends. In the present state of the world, the United States as a leading power bears heavy responsibility to conduct its affairs and to temper its attitudes to maximize international amity and to resolve tensions. The situation was movingly described by George F. Kennan (1981, p. IV-2) in an address given at the time of his receipt of the Albert Einstein Peace Prize:

> Adequate words are lacking to express the full seriousness of the United States' present situation. It is not just that we are, for the moment, on a collision course politically with the Soviet Union, and that the process of rational communication between the two governments seems to have broken down completely; it is also—and even more importantly—the fact that the ultimate sanction behind the conflicting policies of these two governments is a type and volume of weaponry which can not possibly be used without utter disaster for us all.
>
> For more than thirty years wise and farseeing people have been warning us about the futility of any war fought with nuclear weapons and about the dangers involved in their cultivation. Every president from Dwight D. Eisenhower to Jimmy Carter has tried to remind us that there could be no such thing as victory in a war fought with such weapons. So have a great many other eminent persons.
>
> So much has already been said. What is to be gained by reiteration? What good would it now do? Look at the record:

Over all these years the competition in the development of
nuclear weaponry has proceeded steadily, relentlessly, without
the faintest regard for all these warning voices. We have gone on
piling weapon upon weapon, missile upon missile, new levels
of destructiveness upon old ones.

We have done this helplessly, almost involuntarily: like
the victims of some sort of hypnotism, like men in a dream, like
lemmings heading for the sea, like the children of Hamelin
marching blindly along behind their Pied Piper. And the result
is that today we have achieved—we and the Russians together—
in the creation of these devices and their means of delivery,
levels of redundancy of such grotesque dimensions as to defy
rational understanding.

The gravity of the situation is conveyed beyond rhetoric by the decision of Switzerland (a nation noted for its sober objectivity and
practicality) to build shelters to protect its entire population from
nuclear warfare.

Over and against the concept of international amity is the
idea of *patriotism.* Patriotism has many connotations, which range
from absurd national chauvinism to simple love of an accustomed
way of life. The degree of patriotism is usually judged by the acid
test of the willingness of people to bear arms and suffer hardship, if
necessary to die, for their country. International amity and patriotism are interrelated in the sense that an increase of one implies a
decrease of the other. Both, however, have a legitimate place in the
life of a nation. The American people today appear to be at a low
point on the scale of patriotism without at the same time being at a
high point in international amity. It is often said, for example, that
the nation could not now field an effective military force. Responsibility in the area of international relations requires that a sound
balance be struck between international amity and patriotism.

Conclusions: The Informed and Socially Responsible
Citizen and Leader

As a mature industrial country, the United States has clearly
been making significant progress, as progress is usually defined. In
critical areas of the national life, however, there are serious and
intractable problems related to inflation, unemployment, the en-

vironment, crime, drug abuse and alcoholism, the family, the school and neighborhood, the mass media, pressure-group democracy, and war. In all cases these trouble spots reflect insensitivity to the needs of fellow human beings. Basically, they arise from a failure of social responsibility. That glib diagnosis does not, however, imply that any of the problems are easy to overcome. They have proved to be intractable, however, not because the remedies are technically obscure or difficult but rather because they require the acceptance of responsibility by individuals, by groups, and ultimately by society.

To solve these problems, the challenge to higher education is to help produce generations of well-educated graduates who are capable of understanding these problems, who are sensitive to the needs of other people, and who see as their duty the correction of these pressing problems. This is no new task for higher education. Colleges and universities have long cherished the ideal of the *informed and socially responsible citizen and leader.* In recent generations, higher education has slipped away from its traditional role by emphasizing the narrow and technical aspects of disciplines and engaging increasingly in specific vocational training at the neglect of broad learning. The need is to restore and extend the ancient ideal of the well-educated man or woman who is both broadly learned and imbued with social responsibility. These matters will be considered further in later chapters.

Conclusions: The Plight of Youth

A remarkable fact about the ten social problems considered in this chapter is that seven of them are especially applicable to youth. These seven are: unemployment, crime, drug abuse, the family, school and neighborhood, the mass media, and war. Unemployment is concentrated among persons between sixteen and twenty-four years old, crime occurs principally among the young or among persons who began a life of crime when they were young, drug abuse is primarily a phenomenon of youth—even at the grade school level, the problems of the family bear down with special severity on young people and so also do the problems of the school and neighborhood, the deleterious effects of the mass media are most pronounced on young readers, viewers, and listeners beginning almost in the cradle, and the risks and hardships of war strike young people with special severity.[1] These problems, of course, do not afflict all youth equally, but some of them cut across all classes of society and few youngsters are totally exempt. The mere recital of these problems suggests that contemporary America is not a hospitable place for children and youth. One could hardly make a harsher condemnation of any society.[2]

The challenge to our colleges and universities from these youth problems arises because the main function of higher education is the nurturing of youth. It carries out this function not only through its direct teaching of young men and women who will be the citizens and parents of the future but also through its research and human development, its training of the teachers and other professionals who serve youth, and its production of educational textbooks and teaching materials. Higher education is interested also because the prior preparation of its students is determined by what happens in the family, in front of the television set, in the neighborhood, and in the school. The success of higher education in turning out well-educated and socially responsible men and women rests heavily on the prior experiences of its students.

[1]The Surgeon General of the United States, in commenting on the steadily improving health of the American people, remarked that death rates have dropped since 1960 for every age group except those fifteen to twenty-four (*Los Angeles Times*, December 6, 1980, p. I–3).

[2]Two shocking surveys of the plight of the youth are worth reviewing. They are: Johnston, Bachman, and O'Malley, 1980; and the Robert Johnston Company, Inc., 1980.

Education in a Democracy

5

As men become modern men, they are emancipated and thus deprived of the guidance and support of traditional and customary authority. Because of this, there has fallen to the universities a unique, indispensable and capital function in the intellectual and spiritual life of modern society. I do not say that the universities today are prepared to perform this spiritual and intellectual function. What I do say is that a way will have to be found to perform these functions if the pursuit of the good life, to which this country is committed, is to continue and to be successful. . . . The modern void, which results from the vast and intricate process of emancipation and rationalization, must be filled, and . . . the universities must fill the void because they alone can fill it.

—Walter Lippman (1966, p. 17)

This chapter is concerned with the place of *values* among the objectives and outcomes of American higher education. It deals with the opportunity and responsibility of colleges and universities for the moral growth of their students and for propagation of those values that underlie a free society. The thesis is that higher education should be directed toward the growth of its students as whole persons. It should be concerned, of course, with the cognitive learning and the practical competence of its students. But higher education should also be concerned with growth in the moral, religious, emotional, and esthetic aspects of their lives.

Note: Parts of this chapter are based on Bowen (1976) and are included here with the kind permission of the American Council of Life Insurance.

69

No theme runs more persistently through the literature of educational philosophy from the time of the Greeks to the present. Plato quotes Socrates as saying, "And we shall begin by educating the mind and character, shall we not?" In our time, Alexander Heard (1973, p. 16) wrote, "our first concern is the human intellect, but our ultimate concern is the human being. . . . Involved are the development of standards of value, a sense of civic responsibility, the capacity for religious reconciliation, skills, understanding, a sense of purpose, and all the rest required to be a well-integrated person." However, these sentiments are not universally accepted in theory, much less in practice. To develop the argument for including values among the goals of education calls for an inquiry into the fundamental nature of a free society with a capitalist economy and a democratic government.

As we were reminded during the bicentennial year, America is very much a product of the late eighteenth century. The drafting of the Declaration of Independence in America and the publication of Adam Smith's *The Wealth of Nations* in Britain occurred in the same year, 1776. This coincidence was not accidental. These two documents, and later the Constitution of the United States, derived from the same intellectual tradition. The guiding principle was individual liberty, which simply meant minimal intervention by government in the affairs of the people.

Equilibrium

From the standpoint of the economy, the prevailing philosophy of the eighteenth century was that of *laissez-faire*, which meant that people would be free to choose their vocations, to invest their capital, to decide on their rate of saving, and to spend their incomes as they wished without governmental interference. Adam Smith, the great exponent of laissez-faire, argued that under these conditions of freedom the motive of self-interest and the check of competition would result in the best use of resources and a maximum of welfare. He said that although people intended only their own gain they would be led by the invisible hand of God to promote the welfare of society. Then he said in one of his most famous passages, "The statesman who should attempt to direct private people in what manner they ought to employ their capitals would not only load himself with a most unnecessary attention but assume an authority which could safely be trusted, not only to no single person but to no council or senate whatever, and which would nowhere be so dangerous as in the hands of a man who had folly and presumption enough to fancy himself fit to exercise it" (Smith [1776], 1976, vol. 1, p. 456).

The corresponding philosophy as applied to government was that the state would be essentially limited to the protection of life and property, the provision of certain elemental public services (such as roads, schools, a monetary system, and post offices), and the establishment of basic laws concerning especially the acquisition of property and the freedom of persons. The state was to be restrained by checks and balances that would curb arbitrary power and headlong change. Any individual or group would be able to pursue its interests through the political process—working through propaganda, persuasion, and organization. Government then became a kind of marketplace or arena where the competing interests would be balanced against one another and action would occur only when coalitions could be formed that would command an appropriate majority.

For both the economy and the government, the underlying theory was that out of the rivalry of competing interests an equilibrium representing the best resolution of the contending forces would spontaneously emerge. In the case of the economy, an elegant theory susceptible to mathematical analysis was developed that purported to prove that market equilibrium would maximize social welfare. The basis of this elegant theory was that economic values are expressible in money and therefore can be quantified. In the case of government, there were no ready-made measures of welfare and so the theory was less elegant or perhaps less persuasive, yet there was an underlying faith in the theory of a beneficent equilibrium. This faith was based on the concepts of group initiative and countervailing power. The assumption was that when any group saw a chance to gain advantage or to rectify a grievance, it would press its claim; in doing so, it would run into the competition of other groups. Thus, a kind of equilibrium would emerge such that the benefits of society would be reasonably apportioned among the various claimants (Agresto, 1981). The same theory extended to the idea of a balance of power among nations was less elegant and less persuasive than the theory of countervailing power within nations. Yet, given the state of world order, it was accepted as the only available option, and safety was believed to reside in equilibrium and to be threatened whenever the balance was upset.

These theories of equilibrium were all designed to maximize the freedom of individuals, groups, or nations and to resolve competing claims in a market or an arena where they could be balanced off against one another. The process was conceived to be spontaneous and automatic. The motive power came from the self-interest of individuals or groups and the restraint from competition.

Computers. In these equilibrium theories, society functions through mechanisms analogous to computers. Data are fed into the computers by individuals or groups, and the computers "solve" the problem by working out the equilibrium conditions. In the case of the economy, the market serves as the computer, the market being a neutral mechanism that allocates the resources and distributes the income *according to the values the participants bring to the process.* In the case of government, the political system is a neutral arena, also like a computer, that allocates social benefits *according to the values fed into the computer by the participants.* (In international relations, the process is comparable.) In both cases, the government's role is that of neutral proprietor of two computers.

The system is automatic and spontaneous; miraculously, as if by the "invisible hand of God," it produces an equilibrium that yields maximum social welfare. The system requires no specific goals, no forethought or planning, no underlying philosophy, no morality, and no sense of community or common purpose. It calls upon each individual or group to identify personal interests without regard for the general welfare and to press actively for these interests. It requires of the government only to police the basic rules of the game and to see that the computers—the market and the political process—are running smoothly. The job of the politician, as part of the political process, is to be acutely sensitive to what the interest groups want, to be a broker among them in forming coalitions, and to facilitate the achievement of equilibrium. He need not have policies; he need only keep his fingers on the public pulse, a task that in

recent times has been automated by the invention of public opinion
polls.

What I have presented is, of course, an oversimplified carica-
ture of reality. Yet, it describes the underlying theory of the actual
social system not only in the United States but also in most countries
having capitalism combined with political democracy. This system
is simple because it is spontaneous and automatic. The load of
conscious decision making it thrusts upon the government is small.

Economic Problems

Historically, the trouble with the economic system of laissez-
faire was that it left many serious problems unsolved. There was no
built-in immunity from monopoly, and the allocation of resources
and the distribution of income were therefore distorted in comparison to the competitive equilibrium. The system had no built-in
protection against inequality of access based upon race, sex, religion, and national origin. It provided inadequate protection of the
health, safety, and dignity of workers and was not sufficiently attentive to the potential human satisfactions from work. It produced
wide disparities in the distribution of income, and it had no system
for taking care of families without adequate income. The system by
itself could not deliver stability of employment and prices. Finally,
it was subject to a massive case of what logicians call the fallacy of
composition. When everyone pursued his own individual interest,
the result in the aggregate was not maximum social welfare but a
congeries of problems such as unemployment, inflation, overpopu-
lation, urban blight, crime, wastage of natural resources, pollution,
and widespread personal alienation.

As if these problems were not enough, another emerged that
was even more fundamental, namely, the dubious "quality" of
many of the values the people presented to the economy as they
registered their demands upon it. The function of the economy was
to respond to whatever values were brought to it, not to screen the
values it served or to elevate them. Rather, it was expected to be
morally and ethically neutral and to respond by producing whatever
anyone was willing to pay for. The key phrase was "consumer sovereignty." It was up to the family, the church, the school, the mass

media, and general cultural norms to shape the values to which the economy would cater. The system was dependent on the strength of these institutions. As John Adams wrote in his *Diary*, "[The virtues of the New Englanders are formed through] their town meetings, [military] training, town schools, and ministers. . . . These shape their temperance, patience, fortitude, prudence, and justice, as well as their sagacity, knowledge, judgment, taste, skill, ingenuity, dexterity, and industry" (in Agresto, 1981, p. 3).

But the outcome—despite the efforts of family, church, and school—was a predominantly materialistic and acquisitive set of values. The chief goal of individuals came to be that of maximizing the values that could be obtained with money. And that objective was translated into the predominant societal goal, growth of the GNP. Moreover, as it turned out, the economy did not remain neutral in the realm of values but developed its own powerful apparatus of communication in the form of selling and advertising. This apparatus, by constantly advocating materialistic values, may have overwhelmed the moral influence of family, church, and school. Indeed, some people argue that advertising and selling subverted the very principle of consumer sovereignty and that the economy shaped the values of consumers rather than responding to values derived from outside the economy. These issues about the effects of advertising and selling are controversial, but undoubtedly the actual values to which the economy was expected to respond were predominantly materialistic.

I have referred to the economy as a computer. One of the standard remarks about computers is that the printout is only as good as the data fed in. The colloquialism is "garbage in—garbage out." The same thing is true of an economy. Its output is only as good as the values fed into it. One of the most telling criticisms of our economy—vividly illustrated in our television commercials, in printed advertising, and in the ways of life we see about us—is that our wonderful computer has directed our limited resources to the production of a great deal of garbage.

Political Problems

The agency at hand to cope with the economic problems was the government. By resort to the political process, it was argued, every group with a proposal or a grievance could press its claims and counterclaims. Through the competition of all the claimants, an equilibrium embodying the "public interest" would be reached.

As the government was loaded with increasing responsibility for policy making and administrative decision making, social affairs became more complex. Today, this complexity produces the frustrating sense of indecisiveness, stalemate, and unsatisfactory compromise that we all experience. But the political system suffers from other infinitely more disabling maladies.

First, influence in the political process is distributed unequally for reasons relating to the distribution of wealth, education, information, connections, personal persuasiveness, and access to the media.

Second, a political system that responds primarily to the values of various interest groups and seeks an equilibrium among competing forces is likely to be short sighted. The time horizons of interest groups are likely to be fairly short relative to the historical continuity of societies.

Third, a political and economic system that responds mainly to the self-seeking of individuals or interest groups and plays them off against each other rewards aggressive and selfish behavior by its citizens and gives weak encouragement to cooperative behavior rooted in a sense of community and directed toward the broad public interest. The people are thus conditioned to regard society as an arena for self-seeking rather than a collectivity of mankind toward which individuals have responsibilities to give and to serve. The maximization of private income becomes the object of both the economy and the polity, and the *summum bonum* of the society is growth of the GNP, which is merely the sum of the incomes of individuals. The outer limit of our most high-minded statesmanship resides in the belief that if only America produced more and more goods and services at stable prices the welfare of the people would be maximized and all other domestic problems would automatically vanish. Yet, as E. F. Schumacher (1973, p. 27) warned, "An attitude to life which seeks fulfillment in the single-minded pursuit of wealth—in short, materialism—does not fit into this world, because it contains within itself no limiting principle, while the environment in which it is placed is strictly limited."

Fourth, a political system conceived as a computer that responds to the demands of interest groups, whatever they may be, is likely to be a victim of the "garbage in—garbage out" syndrome. For example, the political process in the United States responds to a host of miscellaneous groups such as the American Rifle Association, Sierra Club, Home Builders Council, AFL–CIO, National Association of Manufacturers, American Council on Education, the electric utilities, the American Indians, the Farm Bureau, the military, and thousands of others. The values that these groups bring to the process determine what will come out of it. On the whole they are materialistic values similar to the ones that actuate the economic system. The question that the computer is solving is: Who gets how much of what? The import of this question was aptly explained by Ralph Ketcham (1976), editor of the Franklin and Madison papers, who said:

> Obviously, the framer [of this question] considers government a device for deciding how to parcel out gratification among clashing individuals and groups. That there is no agreed upon or even debatable concept of a good society is, of course, assumed—just grasping and conniving. There is but one justification for the existence of the state under such a "political theory": if it ceased to exist, division of the spoils would be more troublesome and turbulent. The founding fathers, of course, would have understood that to decide "who gets how much of what" was *one* function of government, but they would also have been appalled at any implication that the state had no other purpose. Their climate of opinion insisted that many other questions be asked, and that men and societies seek answers to them out of the moral and social heritage of the classical, Christian, and Augustan world views.

The multiplicity of pressure groups not only leads to contentious "grasping and conniving" but also threatens to undermine majority rule. Our government is on the verge of becoming a "pressure-group state" subject to the veto power of single issue interests or governed by shifting coalitions based on these same interests.

Values: The Missing Ingredient

Adam Smith was a social philosopher, and many of the founding fathers were schooled in social philosophy. They well understood that a society of freedom that would be essentially spontaneous and automatic would be only as good as the values fed into it. They took for granted the values supplied by classical, Christian, and Augustan philosophies. To form these values, they relied on the several educational institutions of society, especially the family, the church, the school, and the college; the outcomes were dependent on the strength of these institutions. In particular, the founding fathers had great faith in education. In describing the thinking of the founding fathers, John Agresto (1981, p. 3) wrote:

> Political life could contribute *something* towards moderating the passions of democratic man. . . . The rest of the campaign for character development would have to be tackled outside of politics: The self-concerned actions of free men would have to be moderated not by law or command but by the moral suasion of economic, familial, educational, and religious institutions. It was the power of these social forces that would help deflect the desire for gain from becoming mere avarice, prevent independence from becoming atomistic individualism or the narrow love of self, and turn the love of individual liberty into a defense of the liberties of all one's fellows. . . . Unfortunately, while liberty and the love of private right have, by any calculus, increased in America over the years, the nonpolitical institutions that supported the formation of moral character are today a good deal weaker.

In the recent disillusionment with the workings of our democratic political system, we sense that the source of our difficulty lies in the values that actuate the economic and political system. Values are the organizing principle of public policy just as they give direction to personal conduct. The actual values that are the basis of our public policy are not consistent with our better natures, not in accord with the authentic values embodied in the teachings of wise thinkers of all ages, and not conducive to the long-range public interest. We sense that there is no way in a free-enterprise economy and a democratic polity to achieve a good society merely by seeking materialistic values through "grasping and conniving." Moreover, we sense that the rivalry among competing claims often results in a stalemate, or in compromises satisfactory to no one, or in short-sighted expediency. And so in frustration we call for charismatic leadership and are frustrated when all we get are politicians who are mere mediators among conflicting interest groups and who are ready to serve any coalition that will produce a majority. Then, in our disillusionment with democratic political leadership, we flirt with various totalitarian solutions. When we cannot quite bring ourselves to accept the totalitarian way out, because we know that in practice it invariably involves a loss of freedom, we then wistfully search for expedients that will preserve the freedom we cherish, will promote the elevated values we long for, and will produce the order and decisiveness that would relieve us of the sense of intolerable stalemate.

The Role of Education

It has been said that Marx tried to reform society by changing social institutions, and Jesus tried to reform society by changing the hearts of men. In the same vein, the choices before us are to change the structure of our society in a totalitarian direction or to alter the values of our people. We reject the totalitarian way because we prize freedom more than order. We believe "that only freedom can permit the human spirit to evolve to its next higher destiny" (Bailey, in Brown, 1977, p. 46). Then we are faced with the solution of Jesus and of virtually all the other great religious teachers. This solution is to change the hearts of men, that is, to change the values they try to seek through the economy and the government. If the values fed into the economic and political computers are worthy values, the market economy and the political system will respond to them. The computers may not be perfect, but they are remarkably responsive to the will of the people as they spend their money and as they vote and exercise political persuasion.

The chief instruments available for the purpose are our various educational institutions. These are chiefly the media of mass communications, the workplace, the family, the school, the church, and the college or university. Of these, the media and the workplace have been almost totally co-opted by the economy and are busy reinforcing the prevailing values. The family also has been partially subverted by the economy and is certainly a weaker source of social responsibility than it once was. Indeed, in large segments of the population, the family has become a negative rather than a positive influence on the development of the goals and behavior patterns of children. The school has fallen on uncertain times. The influence of the church has also waned, though there are signs of renewed religious interest—especially in the growth of evangelical and charismatic approaches to religion and of Eastern religious thought and practice.

This leaves the colleges and universities. They too are partial captives of the prevailing values of society. Many people expect them to be supportive of this value system, and many believe that their chief function is to prepare specialized workers who will fit into particular slots in the labor force. However, the academic community has an ancient tradition of liberal learning. The specific purpose of such learning is to free the mind, to encourage inquiry, to consider the great moral and social issues, to promote a philosophical cast of mind, to cultivate the arts and literature as sources of humane values, and to foster understanding of the world of science and politics. Liberal education is today on the defensive. Each year it occupies a relatively smaller part of the higher educational enterprise as student enrollments steadily shift toward vocationally oriented studies. However, in virtually all colleges and universities, public and private, the liberal tradition survives, and there is a continuing effort to combine liberal learning with vocational preparation. Moreover, despite efforts of the public and their representatives to bring higher education under the control of the "system," the traditional separation of university and state has survived and the essential freedom of the academy has been maintained. The university also continues to have substantial influence over primary and secondary education because it trains the teachers, writes the books, and conducts the research and development for the lower schools.

If the media and the workplace have been irretrievably co-opted by the system, if the family and the school are weak, and the role of the church is still problematical, then higher education may be a strategic point of leverage in modifying the values that actuate the system. A revival of liberal learning for both young people and adults may be an effective means of reorienting the values that propel our economy and our government. This revival would require increasing enrollments in appropriately liberal programs, expanding emphasis on liberal learning in connection with vocational programs, and providing extracurricular opportunities for students that would complement these efforts.

The role of the college or university is particularly critical because it educates virtually all the people who are destined for leadership in our society in the professions, business, and politics. Its main duty should be to prepare the leaders of our country through sound liberal learning not only when they are young but also intermittently throughout their lives. Said more simply, it is the duty of colleges and universities to turn out well-educated men and women for the leadership of the nation.

The college or university, because of its comparative freedom and influence, is the place to begin an effort toward value improvement, but it is not the place to stop. Education in such subjects as history, geography, and literature, and knowledge of skills underlying these subjects occurs in the lower schools and needs strengthening there. Educational television, which has made enormous strides, needs support for reaching larger audiences and perhaps greater freedom in dealing with controversial issues. The church and the new religious movements could have much to offer and need encouragement. Perhaps most important of all, a determined effort is needed to extend early childhood education and to provide appropriate education and work experience for the many teenage youth whose lives are being sacrificed by the lack of both meaningful education and purposeful work.

It is only as we improve our people that we can hope to improve our society. Any realist will have no illusions about the perfectability of human beings or about the possibility that they will, through education, all come to share noble values. But our people and our society are improvable. Indeed, the increasing concern in our society in recent decades about problems such as poverty, pollution, racial injustice, and urban blight, is a product of our widespread education. It is no accident that many of these problems were first rediscovered on our campuses or that students were among the first to agitate about them. As people are sensitized through education to the inconsistencies between the basic values acknowledged by the great thinkers and prophets of all ages and the realities of American society, they will use the economic and political computers to produce new and different answers. And the computers will respond.

Conclusions

The problems of capitalism and democracy can be ameliorated only marginally by modifying the structure of the economy and the government but can be improved primarily by elevating and enriching the values that propel the economy and the government. This improvement can be accomplished only through education broadly defined—especially liberal education. And the leadership in this educational task should be assumed by the colleges and universities. To succeed in this task, they must be able to avoid domination by the same values that have subverted the media, the workplace, and, to some extent, the family and the school. They must be free to cultivate uninhibited and inquiring minds, humane values, and understanding of social and moral issues. They must not serve merely as purveyors of lifelong meal tickets, or socializers, or pillars of the establishment. Rather, they must try to change the values of people—not by indoctrination but by the enlargement of horizons that flow from true liberal education.

The theme, of course trite, is that in education lies the main hope for the good society. It is a theme that was advanced with special force by Thomas Jefferson and John Dewey. It was epitomized by H. G. Wells when he said: "Human history becomes more and more a race between education and catastrophe" (1925). It is also, in a sense, a modern version of Plato's concept of the philosopher-king—except that in a democracy in the twenty-first century every man and woman will be a king or queen. A government of the people, by the people, for the people is only as good as the people.

Higher Education and Social Change

6

✤✤✤✤

It's the direction given by education that is likely to determine all that follows."

—Plato, *The Republic*

Education is the fundamental method of social progress and reform. . . . Through education society can formulate its own purposes, can organize its own means and resources, and thus shape itself with definiteness and economy in the direction in which it wishes to move."

—John Dewey (In Archambault, 1964, pp. 437–438)

Does higher education have the freedom and the nerve to influence human beings according to its own inner standards and values? Or must it merely adjust to the demands of the economy and polity by serving as a purveyor of compliant workers to fit the needs of the labor force, of self-indulgent consumers to fit the prevailing styles of life so skillfully portrayed by Madison Avenue, and of obedient citizens to become pillars of the prevailing political establishment? In considering these questions, let us refer again to eighteenth century history.

Liberty, as conceived in the eighteenth century, rested on two assumptions: (1) that the economy would respond to the free choices of people as they selected their jobs, invested their capital, and exercised their preferences as consumers and (2) that the government would respond to the free choices of people as they voted and engaged in political persuasion. For the values to be supplied by the economic and political establishment would have been as contrary to the spirit of liberty as though the values had been supplied by a totalitarian regime. The distinction between capitalistic-democratic societies and totalitarian societies lies precisely in the source of the values served. In the former, the economy and the polity respond to the freely chosen values of the people as expressed in the market and in the political arena. In the latter, the values are supplied and enforced by a ruling oligarchy.

In theory at least, the values were to be derived mainly from the workings of various independent educational institutions: the family, the church, the school, the college, and the printed media. The first four of these were regarded as responsible institutions with an authentic tradition, a humane outlook on life, and keen moral sensibility. Every family, every church, every school, or every college was not expected to embrace identical values. Rather, conflicting values were to be reconciled partly through the power of tradition, partly through divine revelation, and partly through scholarly inquiry. In the case of the printed media, it was recognized that they would inevitably present conflicting values, which would be subject to public discussion and debate and to the commentary of social critics.

Special provisions were made to establish and guarantee the independence of each of these institutions so that they would not be subverted by the economy or the government. The family was protected mainly by the traditional freedom of parents to rear their children as they pleased subject only to laws concerning gross child abuse and (later) to laws requiring school attendance. The church was insulated from government by the explicit constitutional doctrine of the separation of church and state. Schools were given the protection of local neighborhood control with lay governing boards having the power to levy taxes. The colleges were accorded autonomy through the constitutional right of free speech and the tradition of academic freedom, and these were reinforced by a system of governance in which lay boards served as buffers between the colleges and their sources of financial support. Finally, the mass media—which today includes newspapers, films, radio, television, and also individuals and organizations that wish to spread information or to persuade—received their independence through the constitutional rights of free speech and freedom of the press. These elaborate protections were meant to ensure the independence of the institutions devoted to education, value formation, and value transmittal. They proclaim the importance the founding fathers assigned to the various educational institutions and to their independence.

As indicated in Chapter Five, not all of these institutions have been able to live up to eighteenth century expectations regarding their independence, their influence, or the quality of the values they espouse. The family and the church have almost certainly become less influential than the founding fathers would have anticipated— though the church (in its many forms) may currently be staging a comeback. The school has lost autonomy to statewide and national political control far beyond what the founding fathers could have foreseen, and for other reasons the influence of the school in the realm of values may have waned. The college has probably become more influential than eighteenth century observers would have expected, though the forces of government and the economy are bearing down on it increasingly. The mass media have been largely co-opted by the economy and have become much more ubiquitous and more powerful than our eighteenth century forebears could have imagined. The whole structure that was designed to separate the educational and value-related institutions from the economy and the polity is today in some disarray (see Agresto, 1981). We appear to be following a trend which, if continued, would end in a gradual and silent takeover of all the educational and value-transmitting institutions by the economy and the government—a depressing outlook. If the educational and value-transmitting institutions were consigned increasingly to the role of servants and adjuncts of the economy and polity, if their main function became that of socializing people to fit into the economic and political establishments, liberty might still exist in form, but it would be destroyed in reality. This kind of takeover would be tantamount to a totalitarian revolution. It would be more subtle and therefore in some ways more dangerous than the kind of totalitarianism that arrives in bloody revolutions. However, the structure of educational independence erected by the founding fathers still exists. It is deeply imbedded in law and in tradition. There is still a great deal of healthy independence among our people and no shortage of conflicting opinion and debate. Among the various educational institutions, the colleges and universities may be the strongest. They still enjoy substantial autonomy and still maintain an influential tradition of liberal learning. Moreover, they have close ties to the other educational and value-transmitting institutions. They educate their leaders and conduct much of their scholarship and research. Because of their relative strength, colleges and universities have a special responsibility to reestablish their traditional role in society's quest for worthy values. Higher education may be the premier place in our society that is capable of effective leadership and sustained independent effort in the realm of values.

But does higher education have the freedom, the ability, and the will to assert its traditional values—subject as it is to mounting governmental control, dependent for much of its finances on the choices of students, and deeply implicated in narrowly specialized and technical learning? Or is higher education destined to be mainly adaptive to external pressures and to be the servant of values from outside rather than the independent generator of values from the inside?

Sources of Influence

Despite mounting external pressures, higher education is not without independent influence and this influence could be expanded. It derives from several interrelated sources: the inherent functions of teaching and research, the wide diffusion of overt control over higher education, and the strength that lies in the solidarity of the higher educational system.

Teaching and Research. The colleges and universities of America reach nearly half of each population cohort. In any given year, they are in touch with about 12 million students—most of them at an impressionable stage of life. The students include virtually all of the future leaders of the nation in business, government, the professions, and the arts. Also, the colleges and universities conduct a major part of the basic research and scholarship in our society. In carrying out their teaching and research, they employ a considerable share of the nation's intellectual talent. It would be possible, of course, to conduct this teaching and research at the behest of the economic and political establishment. Even in that event, however, it could not be said that higher education was without influence but only that its influence was exerted in behalf of the status quo. Most colleges and universities do, however, adhere to a rather special ethos, which has been handed down to them through long tradition and which they communicate to their students and to the public with varying amounts of success. Most try to implant in their students certain values or ideals that are associated with the educated man or woman. This ethos is usually not promulgated officially, it is not necessarily shared by all members of the academic community, it often differs from views prevailing among the general public, and it changes over time. (See Bowen, 1977, chap. 9, pp. 267-269. See also Trow in Educational Testing Service, 1974; Miller and Orr, 1980.) Yet one can say that, in any given period, the weight of academic influence is directed toward a particular cluster of values and toward a particular world outlook. In our time, the prevailing ethos of higher education includes several basic ideals that influence the values of its students and that through them bring about social change.

The free mind is a foremost ideal of contemporary higher education. Great importance is attached to freedom of thought and communication, to the obligation to seek the truth through untrammeled inquiry, to tolerance of new and different ideas, to a disposition to explore and to experiment, and to a willingness to break away from conventions, traditions, superstitions, folklore, and myths. Tolerance is considered essential because knowledge is always contingent, ambiguous, complex, and therefore provisional. Emphasis is also placed on rationality, skeptical detachment, and scrupulous intellectual integrity. However, the vogue of logical positivism is on the wane, and intuition, revelation, criticism, and other avenues to the truth are gaining in acceptance.

Closely associated with the ideal of the free mind is the concept of individuality—the ideal that each person should be able to develop according to his or her unique talents and interests. Also related to the free mind is the ideal of historical and geographical perspective. The academic community considers one of its main duties the preservation of the history of events, thought, and art and continual reinterpretation of this history in relation to the present. It seeks to cultivate in its students a sense of history and of historical perspective. Similarly, it encourages geographical cosmopolitanism, including a world outlook, a sense of cultural relativity, appreciation of different cultures, and international understanding.

Another ideal of the academy is a humane outlook, expressed especially in broad social consciousness, social responsibility, and motivation toward betterment of the human condition. In recent years, the humane ideal has been extended to give greater weight to human equality, to promote amicable relationships among classes and races, and to discourage prejudice or discrimination based on sex, race, and religion. The academic community also usually favors the recognition of individual merit based on excellence of performance and the selection of people for various roles according to their qualifications. These meritocratic tendencies, however, exist in tension with the more recent egalitarian tendencies.

The academic community inclines to be concerned with social issues and problems, engages in the study of them, and encourages free discussion of them. Tocqueville, with his usual prescience, wrote (quoted in Kristol and Weaver, 1976, p. xviii): "Among all civilized peoples, the study of politics creates, or at least gives shape to, general ideas, and from those general ideas are formed the problems in the midst of which politicians must struggle, and also the laws which they imagine they create. Political theories form a sort of intellectual atmosphere breathed by both governors and governed in society, and both unwittingly derive from it the principles of their actions." In recent years, the academic community has become more closely linked to the world of social affairs through internships and work study programs, through consulting relationships, through increasing emphasis on the study of public policy, and through greater participation in social criticism. These tendencies sometimes have threatened to compromise the objectivity of the academy. Because it places a high value on leadership, the academic community equips some of its students for leadership roles and also motivates them to assume such roles. In connection with social issues, the academic community has helped lead the way toward public concern for particular issues such as the Vietnam War, human inequality, and environmental deterioration.

On the whole, the academic community stands for excellence in the arts and literature. It does not hesitate to commend Homer or Beethoven or Picasso over artists of lesser gifts. And it regularly practices critical discrimination with reference to recent works of art and literature.

The ideals of the academy are mostly radical ideals. Insofar as they are practiced, they are disturbing to superstition, prejudice, provincialism, ignorance, and discrimination—the enemies of change. They are not the ideals of an educational system that is intended to buttress the status quo by merely socializing its students. They are the very ideals which, if communicated to intelligent and energetic people, are likely to produce social change. On the other hand, the ethos of the academy is rooted in American political and social tradition and does not ordinarily function as a source of violent social revolution.

Not all colleges and universities fully accept these ideals, and those that do are not always effective in transmitting them to their students and to the public. But studies on the educational outcomes of higher education do suggest that college attendance brings about the intended changes to a considerable extent (Bowen, 1977, Chaps. 3–7). Higher education gains influence in proportion to its success in conveying this ethos, that is, in producing enlightened, cultivated, and moral people.

The independent influence of higher education is reinforced by the moral authority that derives from its role in the search for the truth. In this search, part of its responsibility is to be on the leading edge of the new in thought—to conduct research in the spirit of freedom of inquiry, openness to ideas, and pursuit of knowledge for its own sake and without regard to consequences. It is through the sifting and winnowing of ideas, rather than the repetition of dogma, that the truth is found. Another part of its obligation is to serve as the conservator and interpreter of the past experiences of mankind— to study the texts and artifacts of the past with an open mind in the spirit of finding the truth that is in them and interpreting that truth to each new generation. Higher education gains influence in the long run in proportion to its faithfulness to these responsibilities.

As Carl Schorske has observed (in Kaplan, 1980, pp. 103–104), "The university has become a place in which values not only are intellectualized but also are created. Then, intellectualized or no, they flow forth into the culture at large. The university won over the church, and it has become the central institution of the rational society that makes the norms of intellectual progress."

Ultimately, then, the influence of higher education comes from its integrity in hewing to its basic mission, which is to seek the truth and to disseminate it through its teaching and publications. If higher education were merely to adapt to the short-term demands of the economy and the polity and were to neglect its more far-reaching responsibilities in the search for the truth and in the broad cultivation of its students, it would become little more than a cog in the technological machinery.

Diffusion of Control. A second source of independence for higher education is its traditional form of governance. No single person or group or agency sets goals or establishes policy for the higher educational *system.* The individual colleges and universities that make up the system have varied sponsorship. Some are sponsored by the federal government, some by particular states or territories, some by particular local governments, some by religious bodies, and some are simply self-governing independent private corporations. They are financed in varying proportions by the federal government, state and local governments, private foundations, business corporations, private donors, and—not least—students paying tuition. Accreditation is accomplished mainly by voluntary associations of colleges or by professional associations. There is no single or predominant authority over American higher education.

By custom and, to some extent, by law, the governance of individual colleges and universities is on the whole light handed in keeping with a deeply imbedded tradition of institutional autonomy. Virtually all colleges and universities are governed by boards of trustees whose historic function is to serve as buffers between the institutions and the outside world. The boards are designed specifically to ensure freedom of thought and to protect the freedom of the faculties and other officers of each institution to determine what should be taught and learned and how education and intellectual inquiry should be conducted. The function of governance has been deliberately separated from the sources of finance and handed over to trustees. Their assigned role is not that of mere conduit for external pressures from the outside world but rather that of buffer to protect the autonomy and integrity of the institutions and ultimately to oversee the institutions in ways that will best serve the public interest.

Although control is widely diffused and individual institutions are remarkably autonomous, colleges and universities are not exempt from outside pressures. The most significant external influence is the market for students. But institutions are also subject to increasing governmental influence and regulation. Much of this is unnecessary and contrary to well-founded tradition. But on occasion, colleges and universities—even those with high-minded boards of trustees—fall short of serving the public interest and need prodding from the outside. Some of the major innovations in American higher education have come about through outside influences—for example, the land-grant college, the community college, the GI Bill of Rights, various federal research and training programs, and the federal decision to channel financial aid to higher education via students (Niebuhr, 1979). But having indicated that institutional autonomy is not an absolute right and does not always result in the pursuit of the public interest, one may still assert that colleges and universities do in fact enjoy substantial autonomy and that they should have such (qualified) independence.

A System. Despite the wide diffusion of external controls and the considerable internal autonomy of the 3,000 colleges and universities, they do form a coherent higher educational system. And in a cumbersome but effective way this system exerts potent influence over the purposes and activities of individual colleges and universities. The system is not under the control of any person or agency but rather is a largely spontaneous organization. Any observer of the system cannot avoid noticing, however, the pronounced similarities and complementarities among the constituent colleges and universities. To be sure, the institutions differ in size, affluence, admissions criteria, curricula, emphasis on vocational training, attention to advanced study and research, teaching methods, and religious concern. Yet together they make up a remarkably homogeneous and well-ordered system. They are testimony to the efficacy of Adam Smith's "invisible hand."

It is possible for students to receive comparable education in hundreds of institutions in all parts of the country. Students and faculty can easily move about among institutions without serious problems of adjustment. The faculties are mostly the products of graduate schools with strikingly similar objectives and procedures, and the majority of the faculties share a common outlook derived from their education. Institutions tend to emulate one another. Accrediting agencies are inclined to apply about the same standards throughout the country in assessing the worthiness of institutions. Innumerable professional associations assemble faculties and administrators from all parts of the country to exchange information, to discuss common problems, to conduct public relations programs, and to organize political lobbies. Yet there is enough variety among the institutions to serve the needs of a diverse population.

What welds these institutions together is an abstract ideal, widely accepted, as to what higher education ought to be like. This ideal, which is a product of historic experience, is widely shared not only among educators but also among political leaders, students and their families, and the general public. This ideal is part of the common culture of the society, like the law of property or the rules of the highway. Yet, like other parts of the culture, the higher educational system does evolve as it adjusts to changing social conditions. The evolution, however, is usually slow. Established patterns that have received wide acceptance and have met the test of time endure and tend to acquire the sanctity of tradition. The established patterns shelter the individual institutions. They set a model of the way colleges and universities "ought" to be, a model that gives them a certain independence from the demands of government and the market.

The systemic character of American higher education and the constant communication among its parts also means that there exists a true higher educational community, which collectively could wield substantial influence. Not all the institutions speak with a common voice on matters of detail, and unanimity seldom prevails among various sectors of the system even on basic "constitutional" matters. Yet the institutions do have fundamental interests in common, and they do belong to a compelling historic tradition that is far from moribund, though it may have been weakened in recent decades.

Liberal Learning

A major part of the historic tradition was the unyielding insistence that liberal learning, including serious concern for values, should have a central place in higher education. The concept of a "well-educated" man or woman meant a person who had delved deeply into the liberal arts. There was a general agreement in principle, however, that both *liberal learning* and *vocational training* are legitimate and that there should be a reasonable balance between the two. (These terms are defined in the next chapter, in which I use the terms *personal education* and *practical education* in place of liberal education and vocational training.) The controversy has swirled about the word *reasonable*. In the continuing debate on these matters, the weight of academic tradition lay with liberal learning, and the weight of popular opinion (including government, business, and students) lay with vocational training. This debate has been going on for many decades—perhaps even centuries. But in recent years a set of unique conditions involving a radical shift of the balance toward vocational training has weakened the power of higher education. Liberal education has been put decidedly on the defensive. Among the conditions that have contributed to this shift are these:

1. Increasing political control over higher education.
2. Growing financial dependence of institutions on tuitions and formulas for appropriations that are closely related to enrollments.
3. Relative growth of the public sector of higher education.
4. Relative growth of community colleges.
5. Increasing attendance of students from families with limited educational background. These students understandably look to higher education for upward mobility based on good jobs and high pay and tend to elect vocational courses of study.
6. Congestion in the job market because of the entry of the exceptional numbers of youths and women during the 1970s and early 1980s.

The net result of these conditions is that higher education has become increasingly subservient to the demands of the polity and the economy. Its ability to convey the values that flow from the liberal tradition has been substantially diminished. Few colleges and universities have been untouched by these changes. Only a few private institutions and major public universities—mostly well established and affluent or closely affiliated with churches—have escaped. Thousands of institutions have installed new vocational programs or have "vocationalized" old programs, and student enrollments have shifted heavily toward vocational and professional fields. The phenomenon of "students' voting with their feet" and institutions responding mindlessly is scarcely a valid or responsible mode of institutional behavior. As Robert Maynard Hutchins (1936, p. 5) observed, "Most of the things that degrade colleges are done to maintain tuition income."

Despite all these changes, the traditional academic ideal of the liberally educated man or woman has not been forgotten. Indeed, a counterrevolution may be gathering momentum. Many educators are deeply concerned about current trends and are seeking ways to restore the balance between liberal and vocational learning. But in an era of keen competition for students, it is difficult for institutions individually to press the issue without losing enrollments and jeopardizing solvency. To revive and strengthen the influence of liberal learning, there is real need for widespread consultation and concerted action throughout the higher educational system.

In asserting the values that are associated with liberal learning, college and university educators are claiming in effect that their values should have priority over those that flow from government or from the market for students. The traditional autonomy of colleges and universities is defended precisely on the ground that higher education should be able to prescribe values different from those that might be imposed by the body politic if colleges and universities were organized as government bureaus or that might be demanded by individual consumers if educational services were provided by profit-making businesses. But are college and university educators justified in arguing for values different from those of the people in their roles as citizens and consumers? To answer this question candidly is awkward and embarrassing. A valid answer will seem to many to be a display of intolerable arrogance on the part of educators. Yet the question cannot be evaded.

The answer is that people are not qualified to make good judgments about education until after they themselves have been educated. The duty of educators is not to respond supinely to the demands of government or of the marketplace but rather to provide education that people would have chosen had they been educated or would have preferred in retrospect after they had been educated. (This formulation is akin to social contract theory as brilliantly expounded by Rawls, 1978.) The duty of higher education is not to cater to the values that partially educated people bring to colleges but rather to raise the level or quality of these values. The educator is a professional who is entrusted by society to provide appropriate content and method to the end that students will ultimately become well-educated persons. As alumni, they are then able to judge the quality and appropriateness of the education they received. Clearly, the trust that is placed in educators involves heavy responsibility. They could and sometimes do abuse the trust by purveying shoddy education and false values. Therefore, elaborate quality controls operated by the educational community have surrounded higher education. Among these controls are rigorous educational and personal requirements for teachers, voluntary accreditation, informal peer evaluation of institutions, and powerful traditions that influence the way higher education is conducted. That these quality controls have worked reasonably well is indicated by the widespread and consistent satisfaction expressed by alumni concerning their college experiences (Bowen, 1977, chap. 7). However, if educators are to merit the trust that they expect society to grant them, they must be sensitive to the educational needs of society when these needs are viewed by informed and well-educated people. The autonomy granted to educators does not exempt them from social responsibility. As John Dewey so eloquently said, "What the best and wisest parent wants for his own child, that must the community want for all its children" (Archambault, 1964, p. 295).

What Can Be Done?

Can the traditional ideals of higher education be refurbished? Certainly agencies or groups outside higher education—for example, the government, business, the media, the unions, and the churches—are scarcely ready to take the lead in restoring higher education to its traditional role. Some of these groups are unsympathetic, some indifferent, some lacking in understanding, and some powerless. The impetus can come only from higher education itself. How?

Historically, the higher educational community has not been idle in pressing its traditional philosophy. Educators have been vigorous advocates and have used every forum at their disposal to convey the ideal of the well-educated or liberally educated man or woman. They may have done so to the point that their rhetoric has become stale and hackneyed. In recent years, however, the energy and the conviction of educators has diminished. Confronted with a declining population of college-age students, a weak job market for graduates, a financial system based on enrollments, and all this compounded by inflation, educators have felt impelled for sheer survival to compromise their traditional principles by responding to the market for vocational education. Few institutions have been strong enough in student recruitment and finances to resist the pressures.

Much of the higher educational community has thus been placed in a position where it cannot in good conscience advocate one policy while obviously pursuing another. And so the traditionally vigorous advocacy based on principle has often turned either into silence or into dubious apologetics. Under these circumstances, the higher educational community has lost part of its independent influence and has moved some distance toward becoming a mere tool of the economy and the polity rather than an autonomous and independent force. The lost ground cannot be restored easily or instantly. But higher education still has great strengths. On the whole, it enjoys the confidence of the public; it has millions of graduates who are sympathetic; through its trustees, it has close contacts with thousands of influential leaders; it enjoys good rapport with millions of students and staff. It has a firm base on which to build. To set matters aright, several lines of action could be pursued.

First, educational administrators and faculty should give increasing attention to educational philosophy, a subject they have neglected in recent decades. They should think through the complex issues relating to *purpose* in the education of the American people—taking into account both the needs of individuals for personal development and the needs of society for the advancement of the democracy, the culture, and the economy. As things stand in American higher education, administrators are preoccupied with fund raising, budgets, student recruitment, personnel administration, and miscellaneous crises. Faculty are preoccupied with teaching the technical aspects of their disciplines, their research and scholarly interests, and worry about salaries and tenure. The fundamental question of what kind of people they hope their students will become commands little of their time and attention. The kind of educational thinking in the tradition of Plato, Aristotle, Milton, Arnold, Newman, Mill, Dewey, Piaget—to name only a few—has little place on the contemporary American campus. In exploring purpose, all parts of the national higher educational community should work together. Although the proximate purposes of all institutions may not be identical, all types—from Ivy League to community college—share in the responsibility for the widening and deepening of education and for helping to achieve over the generations *a nation of educated people.* Through study and discussion, some agreements might be reached (for all of higher education or at least for various subgroups) that could become foundations upon which public information and political action could be based. Higher education has fallen into the habit of making its case on bread-and-butter arguments—promising to provide people with good jobs and high incomes, promising to produce technological breakthroughs, pleading institutional proverty, saving money for the taxpayers, and the like—and playing down long-term educational benefits to individuals and society. But these generalizations do not apply to all institutions. A promising recent development among educators has been a revival of interest in liberal education. There is much study and discussion of liberal education stimulated in part by the leadership of the Association of American Colleges. Many faculties are actively seaching for ways to strengthen the liberal element in their curricula and instructional methods. These efforts are highly appropriate, and let us hope that they will bear fruit.

Second, educators should give increasing study to the financing and governance of higher education with a view to restoring some of the internal integrity of institutions that was lost when higher education became so heavily dependent on funds delivered directly or indirectly by students. There are many possible ways of reducing this dependence (see Bowen, 1980b, chap. 12) and the higher educational community should be devising specific financial reforms that could be the basis of political action. I am not suggesting that institutional finances could be, or should be, divorced from student enrollments but rather that finances might be better balanced between the broad general needs of institutions and the immediate needs of students than present financial arrangements permit.

Third, educators should be finding ways to help their students appreciate the importance of liberal education. This could be done by guidance, by modifying the way curricula are presented, by combining vocational and liberal material in new ways, and, most of all, by making liberal education interesting, challenging, and applicable to everyday life. Such efforts would be intended eventually to bring about a balance of liberal and vocational elements in the normal curricula. In connection with these efforts, persuasion and education of faculty are also needed. Indeed, much of what is called "faculty development" should be related to the goal of restoring or strengthening liberal education.

Fourth, the higher educational community should be giving serious study to the matter of governance by federal, state, and local authorities with a view to developing standards consistent with academic freedom. Clearly, many public authorities are overstepping the boundaries of academic freedom. Individual institutions are ill prepared to cope with these encroachments. They do not have a set of recognized principles to serve as a guide, and their governing boards are not well informed about their role as buffers between government and the campus.

Fifth and finally, a special responsibility falls on a few elite institutions. Because of their affluence and reputation, they are partially exempt from the pressures bearing down on the rank and file of colleges and universities. These institutions, some private and some public, can attract enough students and sufficient funds that they are not compelled to compromise their standards. Most of them feel financially pinched because their ambitions usually outrun their resources, but they nevertheless are able to serve as models for the rest of the academic community. The whole higher educational system needs such models. Without them, the concept of academic freedom and the kind of education and research associated with it might well disappear. The elite institutions unfortunately tend to be exclusive and to have poor communications and tenuous relationships with the rank and file of colleges and universities, and their role as leaders is therefore less effective than it might be.

Action of the kinds described would require vigorous leadership and money. It would require study and a search for policies appropriate to academic freedom. It would also involve both decisons by individual institutions and concerted political action on the part of the higher educational community.

The history of higher education does not give confidence in the ability of the higher educational community to join in unified efforts. But the crisis is severe enough, and the basic principles of academic freedom and liberal learning are sufficiently threatened that joint action is surely called for. Most of the independent moral influence of higher education lies in its common tradition and in its solidarity.

Toward a
Nation of
Educated People

7

❖ ❖ ❖ ❖

*I have never known anyone who regretted that he became well
educated.*

—Anonymous

Formal education in the United States was first confined mostly to
the elementary school, symbolized by the little red school house.
When the bulk of the population had achieved elementary education, attention was turned to the expansion of secondary schooling.
By the time of World War II, an overwhelming proportion of
younger age groups were attending and graduating from secondary
schools. Then it became higher education's turn. Previously, higher
education had been reserved for a tiny minority—mostly from upper
classes. Following World War II, the educational system was topped
off with a layer of college or university education available to the
masses. The terms *universal higher education* and *learning society*
were invented. They did not mean that every single individual
would become college educated. Rather, they meant that higher
education would be available to all, that no one would be denied
access because of lack of finances, and that higher learning would be
attained by many, possibly a large majority of society. And it was

Note: Parts of this chapter are based on an address given by the
author at the University of Texas on February 4, 1981 and are included here
with the kind permission of the university.

expected that even advanced graduate and professional study would be open to unprecedented numbers. The ultimate goal was *a nation of educated people*. It was an ambitious and open-ended goal to which no country had ever been before aspired, and its full implications were unknown.

So began the exhilarating postwar era of growth in higher education. In the late 1970s, this growth began to level off and there was much talk—even fatalistic acceptance—of falling enrollments. And public opinion was in a mood of skepticism about the value of what had been accomplished and of hesitancy about next steps for the future. Today, the goal of *a nation of educated people*—in whatever way it may be defined—is still far from achievement. At best, many decades—perhaps a century—will be required even to approach it.

The extension of education could be expected to yield many benefits. For example, it could probably be counted upon to increase economic productivity, to enhance national prestige and power, to help reduce violent crime, or to cut down the welfare rolls. These effects are surely desirable and would deserve consideration in any decisions about educational policy. But the basic objective of widening and deepening education would be defensible in its own right without any of these side effects. It could be advocated simply on moral grounds based on three propositions (Bowen, 1977, chap. 15): (1) Substantial education is conducive and essential to the fulfillment of people as whole human beings. (2) The percentage of the population that could achieve personal growth through higher education probably exceeds greatly the percentage now benefiting from it. As of 1980, there is a considerable waste of human potential. Over time, the percentage who could benefit will probably increase. (3) Given these two propositions, each person should have the opportunity, the encouragement, and even the obligation to develop fully his or her unique personal powers insofar as that can be done through education. This argument reduces to the proposition that it is immoral to suppress people's potential by keeping them ignorant. This is, of course, not a new idea. It was the theme of Gray's "Elegy" written in the eighteenth century:

> Perhaps in this neglected spot is laid
> Some heart once pregnant with celestial fire,

Hands, that the rod of empire might have sway'd,
Or wak'd to ecstasy the living lyre.

But Knowledge to their eyes her ample page
Rich with the spoils of time did ne'er unroll;
Chill Penury repress'd their noble rage,
And froze the genial current of the soul.

Full many a gem of purest ray serene,
The dark unfathom'd caves of ocean bear:
Full many a flower is born to blush unseen
And waste its sweetness on the desert air.

Some village-Hampden that with dauntless breast
The little Tyrant of his fields withstood;
Some mute inglorious Milton here may rest,
Some Cromwell guiltless of his country's blood.

The same theme was expressed prosaically by Thomas Carlyle who said, "That there should be one man die ignorant who had the capacity to learn, this I call a tragedy. To impart the gift of thinking to those who cannot think; this one would imagine, was the first function a government had to set about discharging." If to the moral argument the societal benefits are added, the case for extending higher education, so far as practically feasible, becomes overwhelming.

In this chapter, I shall explore the meaning of "a nation of educated people" and in doing so consider the critical question of the potential educability of the population. Much of this chapter is speculative. It reaches no fully documented or final conclusion. But it does lay out in full view some of the most critical long-range issues about the future of education in America. And these issues have urgent implications for those responsible for educational policy in the near future.

The concept of the "well-educated person" is elusive. There are at least four ways of defining it. One is simply to equate it with the baccalaureate degree and thus to imply that all persons who have received the baccalaureate may in some sense be considered well educated; another is to cast the definition in terms of a course of study that would be calculated to produce a well-educated person; a third is to describe the characteristics of a person who can be said to be well educated; and the fourth is to state the definition in terms of the depth of education that a specified proportion of the population could be expected to master. By adoption of all four of these approaches, perhaps the concept can to some degree be clarified.

The Baccalaureate Degree

This degree signifies many things. It usually refers to four academic years of time served or about 120 semester credits earned. For some students, it means a broad liberal education without any training for a specific vocation; for others, it represents specialized vocational training with minimal liberal learning. For some students, it means admission at about age eighteen immediately after high school graduation; for others, it means admission before completion of high school work or many years beyond the age of eighteen. For some, it means almost exclusive attention to required studies; for others, it means unrestricted electives. For some, it indicates full-time studies combined with residence on a campus and participation in a rich extracurricular and social life; for others, it means part-time study with residence off campus and no extracurricular participation. For some, it represents renowned professors, richly appointed libraries, laboratories, and museums, and commodious recreational and social facilities; for others, it represents staff and facilities reeking with poverty.

Despite the wide range of requirements and conditions under which baccalaureate degrees are earned, there is a certain modal concept of that degree. The concept is deeply embedded in the traditions of American higher education. In general, the degree represents completion of a four-year program following a high school "preparatory" program. It involves some breadth of learning among the traditional academic subjects, including the sciences, social studies, and humanities and some modest specialization in a single field or area. The specialization may be in an academic field having no career potential other than teaching the same subject, or it may be in fields such as nursing, engineering, business, or an allied health profession. Even those vocational fields that demand most of the students' time, engineering being the prime example, make obeisances to breadth of learning by requiring students to take a few courses in fields such as English and economics. The course requirements and the guidance afforded students, however, usually steer them toward a diversified program intended to help them to become—over their lives—well-educated and cultivated human beings. The concept of the baccalaureate degree often includes not only the learning of certain subjects but also the broad emotional and moral development and practical competence of students as citizens and as members of families and organizations. Some attention—at least lip service—is given to sound values, esthetic sensibility, religious interest, human understanding, physical skills, and preparation for leisure. These qualities are nurtured partly through the curriculum and partly through extracurricular facilities, programs, and experiences.

The modal concept of the baccalaureate also contains the idea that students will be influenced favorably by faculty role models who exemplify the well-educated woman or man. The particular choice of courses is not as important as the outlook of the teachers and the spirit in which they conduct their teaching. In this connection, it is often observed that subjects usually regarded as appropriate to liberal learning (such as philosophy or literature or chemistry) can be taught in a narrow, pedantic, and technical manner, and that subjects usually held to be narrowly vocational and technical (such as engineering and nursing) may be taught in a manner that yields breadth, perspective, and liberation.

The modal concept of the baccalaureate is helpful but not adequate in defining the well-educated man or woman because in practice the variations from the mode are substantial. As William Bouwsma (Kaplan, 1980, p. 27) has suggested, "The body of requisite knowledge has become so vast that no one can hope to master more than a small segment of it. So in the popular mind, an educated man is now some kind of specialist; and in a sense we no longer have a single conception of the educated man but as many conceptions as there are learned specialties." But the problem of "disconnexion" is not of recent vintage. Wordsworth foresaw specialization as an enemy of the whole human being when he wrote in "The Excursion":

> Viewing all objects unremittingly
> In disconnexion dead and spiritless;
> And still dividing, and dividing still,

Break down all grandeur, still unsatisfied
With the perverse attempt, while littleness
May yet become more little; waging thus
An impious warfare with the very life
Of our own souls!

The Course of Study

A second approach to defining the well-educated person is to sketch out a course of study which, if completed satisfactorily, would set the student on a lifetime journey calculated to make her or him well educated. The course of study to achieve this result would be of two kinds: *personal education,* by which I mean broad development or fulfillment of the whole person, and *practical education,* by which I mean training for work, family life, politics, consumer choice, health, leisure activities, and other practical affairs. The words *personal* and *practical* are akin to but not the same as *liberal* and *vocational.* I have avoided the latter two words because they tend to be imprecise, hackneyed, and laden with emotion. Practical education includes not only vocational education relative to future work but also education intended for other practical affairs.

The distinction between personal and practical education is not clearcut. The overlap is great. Personal education, though primarily designed to enhance each individual as a person, may have important consequences for work and other practical affairs (Bowen, 1978; Chickering, 1981). Practical education, though primarily designed to enhance specific skills of use not only in work but also in other practical affairs, may be influential in the development of the individual personality (Cheit, 1975). Yet the distinction is worth making because of the inclination of the two types of education to get out of balance. In recent times, for example, practical education, especially that related to future careers, has tended to submerge personal education. I do not suggest, however, that practical education is in some sense illegitimate or unnecessary. People understandably want to and should prepare themselves, in one way or another, for work and other practical affairs. Each person should find a vocation (in the sense of "calling") through which he or she would be able to contribute to society something of value. The ideal is a reasonable balance between personal and practical education such that the growth of the person as a human being is not unduly sacrificed to self-centered pecuniary ends. Much of practical education is derived from experiences throughout life, and it should not overwhelm personal education during the school years. To achieve the ideal balance, it is necessary to consider the whole of education—from nursery school through graduate school and beyond, including not only schools and colleges but other educational media as well. Some stages of life or places of education may be more suited to practical education and some more congenial to personal education. It is balance over a lifetime, not necessarily within each semester of a school or college career, that should be sought.

With these preliminary remarks, I shall be specific about the subjects that would make up an education calculated to produce well-educated people—of whom there might someday be a great many. These subjects (not necessarily courses) would constitute a six-year program, two years in high school and four years in college:

I. Personal education
   A. The common core
      1. Language skills including reading, writing, speaking, and, in an era of electronic communication, listening—all in English.
      2. Logic, mathematics, and computer science.
      3. History of Western civilization with special emphasis on the development of democratic institutions.
      4. Philosophy.
      5. Religious studies.
      6. National and world geography with special reference to peoples, cultures, economies, ecology, and relationships.
      7. Foreign languages: not required but with incentives or encouragement such that a substantial minority of persons would elect to study them *in some depth* so that the nation could have contact with many foreign cultures.
      8. Educational opportunities: training and guidance related to opportunities and techniques for lifelong educational use of adult education, radio, television, books, maga-

zines, newspapers, libraries, churches, museums, musical organizations, armed forces, workplaces, unions, clubs, experiential learning, and independent study. As Alfred Whitehead observed (1929, p. 6), "Education is the acquisition of the art of the utilization of knowledge."

9. Career opportunities: the concept of vocation, world of work, and choice of vocation.
10. Physical education and outdoor recreation.

B. Required fields within each of which limited choices of specific courses would be permitted. In each field, emphasis would be on fundamental principles, methods, and great issues.
   1. Natural sciences
   2. The humanities
   3. The fine arts
   4. Social studies

C. The entire program of personal education would be designed to help students acquire a cosmopolitan outlook. This would be achieved partly through the study of world geography and foreign languages as specified, partly through elective courses pertaining to international affairs and foreign cultures, partly through the regular curriculum and the extracurricular life of each institution.

II. Practical education
A. Meeting the requirement of a major field of study in the sciences and arts that might provide the basis for a vocation or for advanced study leading eventually to a vocation; or preparing for a vocation; or through undergraduate study, apprenticeship, on-the-job experience and training, and so on.
B. Preparing for other practical affairs such as interpersonal relations, management of personal business, child development, health, consumer choice, and use of leisure.

In general, the requirements for the portion of the program related to *personal* education would be at a level of rigor such that it could be completed by a qualified student in four years of full-time study—two years in high school and two years in college. And the portion relating to practical education could be completed in two years of full-time study in college.

The reader may reasonably regard this program as boringly conventional, as indeed it is. It seems commonplace precisely because many faculty committees and educational commentators, when they design curricula, produce something similar. It is what most well-educated parents want for their own children. There is in fact wide agreement on the general features of good undergraduate education. The ideal seldom gets translated into actual educational practice, but there is little controversy over the general content and form of the ideal.

In defining the ideal education in terms of a list of subjects and a specified duration of study, I emphatically do not imply that all learning would take place in schools and colleges. Some of it (or for some students, all of it) might occur elsewhere. Neither do I imply that the various parts of the program would occur in a particular sequence. Personal and practical education might occur at different ages for different individuals. The subjects might be combined or integrated in various ways. For many students, practical and personal education might be carried on simultaneously. Moreover, some of each type of education might be worked into extracurricular programs. A wide range of instructional methods and facilities might be employed. Experimentation with new curricula and modes of learning would be possible. Indeed, diversity would be desirable and essential to fit the education to students of varying backgrounds and interests and to avoid the risk of placing all the educational eggs in one basket. The listing of subjects is intended not to lay down a fixed regimen but to be specific about the basic ingredients of the education that would be calculated to produce well-educated people.

Traditionally, the formal curriculum has been expected to be enhanced and reinforced by an environment rich in discussion, interpersonal relationships, cultural amenities, and democratic values. Some of the education would occur by partaking of a suitable environment as well as by attending formal classes. In the days of full-time residential students attending relatively small institutions, it was easy—though not always cheap—to create the appropriate educational environment. But in a time of part-time commuters and huge institutions, it is not so easy to create environments to complement the curriculum. One of the most urgent needs of contemporary higher education is to find ways of creating complementary environments or to make use of suitable cultural resources that already exist in the wider community.

Characteristics of a Well-Educated Person

Defining an educational ideal in terms of a baccalaureate degree or a list of subjects, as I have done, has the merit of specificity but the drawback of not dealing with the underlying spirit and purpose of the education. A given set of subjects can be taught and learned with quite different outcomes depending on the basic qualities of mind, character, and temperament that are sought and on the spirit in which the education is conducted. And these are reflected especially in the relative emphasis given to positive knowledge and to matters of value and in the kinds of persons serving as exemplars.

The educational ideal I have in mind, like all matters of spirit and value, is hard to describe accurately and succinctly.* Nevertheless, I shall make the attempt by describing the characteristics of well-educated persons. These characteristics thus become the goals of education for persons who have the capacity to become well educated. They refer to body, mind, and spirit. In general, educated persons would have acquired the following characteristics:

1. They would be seekers for the truth. They would be open to ideas and emancipated from prejudice and dogma. They would not be swayed by every fad, but would be able to weigh evidence of various kinds and thus to reach independent and sound—though always provisional—judgments about the truth.
2. Their perspective would extend over the past, the present, and the future. They would have a grasp and an appreciation of the social and cultural heritage from which our society is derived, especially of the origins and development of democratic thought and practice. Their active interest in and understanding of the contemporary world would include knowledge of current affairs,

*A book that describes in some detail this educational ideal is *Education and the Common Good*, by Philip H. Phenix (1961). This book can be strongly recommended, not because it lays out a practicable program for baccalaureate education but because it elucidates with great clarity and force the basic ideals toward which such an education should aspire.

social problems, politics, science and technology, the arts, education, and religion. They would have some sophistication about the human condition. They would be attuned to the idea of social change and would be able to adjust to it and also to speculate on possibilities for the future. They would be able to share in a base of knowledge and culture common to well-educated persons. They would have breadth, versatility, and adaptability.

3. They would be citizens of the world as well as of the United States. Their outlook would be cosmopolitan, not merely local or national.

4. They would have achieved a firm moral base embodying at least a sense of vocation, a deep concern for human betterment, the obligation of service to others, social responsibility, equality among persons, and loyalty to the truth. They would have overcome some of the excessive hedonism or self-indulgence that has been a prominent feature of contemporary life.

5. They would have thought in a mature way about the ultimate meanings of human existence.

6. They would have delved in some depth into a particular field of study. This field might be the basis for careers or for advanced study or might simply allow pursuit of particular interests in the spirit of learning for its own sake.

7. They would have had sufficient experience in interpersonal relationships to enable them to get along with other persons with civility, tact, and finesse, to be constructive members of groups and organizations, and to be good companions.

8. They would be self-reliant and self-supporting. They would be prepared to cope not only with making a living but also with practical matters associated with their private lives such as personal business, child development, health, consumer choice, and leisure.

9. They would have the capacity and desire to learn throughout their lives.

10. They would have developed their bodies as well as their intellects and achieved rapport with nature (Stoddard, 1962–1963).

11. They would be prepared to live interesting and fulfilling lives as the human condition and individual fortunes might permit.

Lists of characteristics or goals such as those presented here have been compiled for centuries by hundreds of educational philosophers. Libraries are full of books and articles that lay out high-minded educational ideals. I once perused a great deal of this literature and compiled more than 1,500 goal statements from sources ranging from Plato to Clark Kerr (Bowen, 1977, chap. 2). I found remarkably little disagreement on the goals. Lists similar to the one I have just presented are numerous and command substantial agreement. However, almost all of these lists, including mine, present an ideal for the educated person that far surpasses practical possibilities. They refer to the education of saints, not of fallible and mortal human beings. Certainly, not all these goals could be achieved through a few years of study even in educational programs directed toward affective and moral as well as cognitive objectives and taught by exemplary people.

Among the classic statements of educational goals, the one I like best is that of Cardinal Newman ([1859] 1958, pp. 151–153):

> If then a practical end must be assigned to a university course, I say it is that of training good members of society. Its art is the art of social life, and its end is fitness for the world. It neither confines its views to particular professions on the one hand, nor creates heroes or inspires genius on the other. Works indeed of genius fall under no art; heroic minds come under no rule; a university is not a birthplace of poets or of immortal authors, of founders of schools, leaders of colonies, or conquerors of nations. It does not promise a generation of Aristotles or Newtons, of Napoleons or Washingtons, of Raphaels or Shakespeares, though such miracles of nature it has before now contained within its precincts. Nor is it content on the other hand with forming the critic or the experimentalist, the economist or the engineer, though such too it includes within its scope. But a university training is the great ordinary means to a great but ordinary end; it aims at raising the intellectual tone of society, at cultivating the public mind, at purifying the national taste, at supplying true principles to popular enthusiasm and fixed aims to popular aspiration, at giving enlargement and sobriety to the ideas of the age, at facilitating the exercise of political power, and refining the intercourse of private life. It is the education which gives a man a clear conscious view of his own opinions and judgments, a truth in developing

them, an eloquence in expressing them, and a force in urging them. It teaches him to see things as they are, to go right to the point, to disentangle a skein of thought, to detect what is sophistical, and to discard what is irrelevant. It prepares him to fill any post with credit, and to master any subject with facility. It shows him how to accommodate himself to others, how to throw himself into their state of mind, how to bring before them his own, how to influence them, how to come to an understanding with them, how to bear with them. He is at home in any society, he has common ground with every class; he knows when to speak and when to be silent; he is able to converse, he is able to listen; he can ask a question pertinently, and gain a lesson seasonably, when he has nothing to impart himself; he is ever ready, yet never in the way; he is a pleasant companion, and a comrade you can depend upon; he knows when to be serious and when to trifle, and he has a sure tact which enables him to trifle with gracefulness and to be serious in effect. He has the repose of a mind which lives in itself, while it lives in the world, and which has resources for its happiness at home when it cannot go abroad. He has a gift which serves him in public, and supports him in retirement, without which good fortune is but vulgar, and with which failure and disappointment have a charm. The art which tends to make a man all this is in the object which it pursues as useful as the art of wealth or the art of health, though it is less susceptible of method, and less tangible, less certain, less complete in its result.

Even accepting Newman's disclaimers and adding lifelong learning to school and college programs, his goals are unlikely to be fully attained. They are ideals—impossible dreams. As such they are useful in providing a sense of direction to educators and their students and as criteria for measuring achievement. Stating the ideals is, of course, not the same as achieving them, but it is a beginning.

The course of study and the list of characteristics or goals I have outlined are closely related to some contemporary educational practice—for example in those high schools that adhere to basic studies in their college preparatory programs and in those colleges and universities that emphasize "general education" for undergraduates. Indeed, the institutions that are held in highest esteem are devoted to this kind of education. However, as one compares the proposed education to that offered in 1980 in the rank and file of

American high schools and colleges, glaring differences appear. The proposed program would place relatively greater emphasis on values, would give relatively greater attention to the affective development of students, would direct more attention toward foreign cultures and affairs, and would demand considerably greater intellectual rigor than does the education offered in most contemporary institutions. The question remains: What proportion of the population is, or could be, capable of becoming well educated in the sense that the term has been loosely defined? This question leads to the definition of the well-educated person in terms of the proportion of the population whose potential ability would enable them to become well educated if all the other conditions were favorable.

Educability

In regard to the educational ideals I have suggested, the question is not whether this kind of education would be desirable. Of course it would be. The critical question is whether it would be feasible for a substantial proportion of the population (Premfors, 1979). In the past, such an education has been limited to a small minority, mainly persons from families of above-average wealth and education and other persons of exceptional talent and energy. We have no real knowledge of the proportion of persons who are today well-educated according to the standards suggested.

We do know that of the adult population over twenty-five years of age only about 29 percent have ever attended college and only about 16 percent have graduated. But we have no fix on the number of those who attended college but are *not* well educated or of those who did not attend but *are* well educated. The number of college attenders who are not well educated probably exceeds the number of nonattenders who are well educated. If that is so, one might guess that the percentage of well-educated people in the present adult population is of the order of 10 to 20 percent.

We also know that recently there has been a huge increase in the numbers attending college, until today about 47 percent of each age cohort attends and 28 percent eventually graduate. Thus, in another fifty or sixty years, with attention to quality as well as numbers, the well-educated might constitute 20 to 30 percent—

roughly a quarter of the adult population. This estimate assumes that college attendance and graduation hold steady at present rates (47 and 28 percent respectively), that the character of college education remains about as at present, and that the proportion of nonattenders who become well educated is unchanged. For the percentage to reach this level would be an astonishing achievement. Perhaps no country ever before would have attained such wide dispersion of education. But it would probably still fall far short of the ultimate educational potential of the nation, which I judge to be well over half the population.

To achieve the goal of a majority well educated, even over several generations, would be a miracle. Perhaps it is not reachable. It would involve immense growth in numbers being educated at the college level. And to accommodate these numbers with their varied backgrounds and interests would require substantial changes in the methods and organizations of the educational system. But whether or not such a goal is achievable, those responsible for educational policy cannot properly avoid facing the high probability that a majority of the American people are potentially capable of becoming "well educated" as the term is here understood. Educators cannot responsibly be indifferent to the "mute inglorious Miltons" or to the many more persons of lesser talent who might nevertheless become well educated, but, for a variety of reasons, are held in ignorance. As Martin Luther said (Ulich, 1954, p. 223), "In my judgment there is no other outward offense that in the sight of God so heavily burdens the world, and deserves such heavy chastisement, as the neglect to educate children."

Considerable evidence and authority indicate that the percentage of persons educable at a high level has grown steadily over many years and could continue to grow in the future (Witmer, 1978; President's Commission on Higher Education, 1947). The educability of people is strongly influenced by the economic, social, and cultural condition of their families during the formative years of childhood and youth. Not only does the situation of families exert direct influences upon children but it also affects the character of neighborhoods, peer groups, and schools in which children move and learn. In general, the more impoverished the family background, the less favorable are all these influences. Given the critical importance of family background in the shaping of young people, it is evident that as more favorable economic, social, and cultural conditions are diffused to ever more of the adult population, the environment in which children are reared will be improved. The health and strength of children will be greater, their life experiences in the form of play, hobbies, reading, radio and television, travel, and contacts with peers will, on the whole, be enriched. Their parents will be more sophisticated and more supportive about child development and education and will provide better guidance. Thus, from one generation to the next, an increasing proportion of children will be prepared for advanced education. This result has been documented by the long-term upward trend of IQ scores of the population as tests have been given from one generation to the next and also by the relatively better child care found in homes in which the parents are well educated. Similarly, substantial correlations exist between educational level of parents and IQ or achievement scores of children.

Educability should not be limited to young adults of traditional college age. If there is one thing the experience of the GI Bill and of subsequent programs for older adults has taught us, it is that readiness for higher education does not occur magically at the age of eighteen, and frequently shows up later in life among those who passed up (or were bypassed by) higher education.

In considering the question of educability, however, one cannot depend exclusively on historic data. Perhaps it was true that in the past the diffusion of economic, social, and cultural progress to more and more people resulted in a steady growth of persons prepared for higher education. Perhaps it was once possible to recruit millions of people for our colleges and universities without seriously lowering the average academic ability of entering students. But will it be possible to continue this trend in the future? The well-advertised decline in the College Board SAT and ACT scores suggests that the diffusion of readiness for college may also have slowed down. The widespread problems pertaining to the behavior of youth suggest that familial influences are not working as well as in the past. High school preparation for college has apparently deteriorated. The percentage of the population who *want* education may be falling short of the percentage who could attain it. Perhaps we have reached an impasse in our quest of a nation of educated people.

Yet it is quite clear that the educational task is far from completed. Millions of Americans who are, or could be, educable are not yet in college. Perhaps the most convincing evidence of this comes from the differential rates of college attendance among persons from families of different income levels or socioeconomic statuses (SES). Data on these differences are scarce, but they invariably show the same basic results, namely, that attendance rates vary with income or SES. A few samples of these data are presented in Appendix Table B5. They reveal that among families of high income or SES, two thirds to three fourths of the children attend college, whereas among families of low income or SES, only about one third attend. College attendance among upper-class persons may be a better indicator of potential educability of the whole population than the percentage from all classes of the population attending. It gives some indication of the extent of educability among persons who have the advantage of educated parents, good neighborhoods and schools, security, good nutrition and health care, and stimulating experiences. If all children could have these same advantages, the educability of those of lower SES, and therefore of the whole population, might be raised substantially. (I am not necessarily suggesting that the whole population could achieve the same degree of educability as that attained by the present upper classes.)

There are other evidences that the number of potentially educable persons could be much higher than the numbers now attending college. The percentage of young persons attending college in some states is much less—in some cases half—of that in others. Residents attending college somewhere (not necessarily in the home state) are 45 percent or more of the population of ages eighteen to twenty-four in five states: California, New York, Rhode Island, Massachusetts, and New Jersey. In five other states, the corresponding percentages are 26 or less: Arkansas, Alaska, Kentucky, Louisiana, and Georgia. If the percentage of those eighteen to twenty-four years old attending college in all states were as high as it is in the leading state (California), the total enrollment in all of higher education would increase by about 3.5 million students, or by more than 30 percent. Another indication that the potential is greater than present enrollments (though there are no reliable statistics) is that many well-qualified students of community colleges do not transfer to four-year institutions. Also, when one considers that only 16 percent of adults twenty-five years old and over are college graduates, it is obvious that millions of adults could benefit from higher education. There is no shortage of persons who stand in need of education and could partake of it with benefit. Adult learning is a particularly important device for increasing the numbers of the educated population. Not only does it offer elemental equity for those people who were left out, it also provides a shortcut toward the goal of widespread education.

In a consideration of educability, the question of diversity among learners becomes critical. Not all persons can be run through the same curriculum, the same methods of instruction, and the same time schedule with any hope that half or more will ever reach the goal. Accommodations would be necessary for those who differ in their facility with the abstract versus the concrete, with the rational versus the artistic, with the interpersonal versus the mechanical, with oral versus written communication. There would be need also to accommodate people with and without certain experiences, those who are fast and slow learners, and those who are early and late bloomers. To produce millions of well-educated persons from such variegated material would require considerable flexibility in method (Cross, 1971, 1976). But flexibility in method is not the same as flexibility in purpose. The purpose would remain the same, although, of course, different learners might differ in the extent of their achievement of the purpose or in the internal pattern of their achievement. However, when one of the purposes is to encourage increasing numbers of people to become well educated, some liberality in the definition of purpose is also called for. Such liberality extended to the marginal students would inevitably lead to different standards for different people. I do not find this objectionable if there is reasonable equality of effort among all groups and if the deficiencies in one generation can be rectified in subsequent generations. Because of the tendency of students from families of limited educational backgrounds to elect specifically vocational subjects, it would become especially important that these subjects be taught in a liberal spirit. But if in adjusting to individual differences the concept of the well-educated person were stretched too far, the ultimate goal, a nation of educated people, would be defeated. The pedagogical problem is to take account of people's widely different characteristics and talents, indeed to make use of these characteristics and talents, in leading them toward the goal over several generations.

Perhaps the most ardent and persistent advocate of the objectives I am proposing was Robert Maynard Hutchins, former president of the University of Chicago. A quotation from his book, *The Higher Learning in America* (1936, p. 61), expresses his view:

> I concede the great difficulty of communicating the kind of education I favor to those who are unable or unwilling to get their education from books. I insist, however, that the education I shall outline is the kind that everybody should have, that the answer to it is not that some people should not have it, but that we should find out how to give it to those whom we do not know how to teach at present. You cannot say my content is wrong because you do not know the method of transmitting. Let us agree upon content if we can and have faith that the technological genius of America will solve the problem of communication.

Hutchins's views on educability were extremely optimistic—far more than mine. But he was not alone in expressing the view that educability is widely diffused throughout the population. In fact, this theme runs through much of the literature on higher education.

It should not be surprising that Hutchins's colleague, Mortimer Adler, expressed similar ideas. Adler repeatedly asserted that virtually all people are educable, can aspire to become educated persons, and should be educated (Kaplan, 1980). He was careful to point out, however, that human beings are educable "in different degrees proportionate to differences in their native endowments" (p. 166). He then added that "we have not yet been able to discover ways of helping the smaller receptacles get their proportionate share of the same substance. The operative words here are 'not yet', . . . we have not yet given sufficient time, energy, and creative ingenuity to inventing the means for doing what has never been done before" (Kaplan, 1980, p. 169).

In the same vein, Mark Van Doren (1959, p. 28) in his book on *Liberal Education* asks, "How many educated persons should there be? . . . How many can there be? Nobody doubts that there should be as many as possible, but estimates of possibility range high and low." No human being, he says "should miss the educa-tion proper to human beings" (p. 29). Education is for all: "A democ-racy that is interested in its future will give each of its members as much liberal education as he can take, nor will it let him elect to miss that much because he is in a hurry to become something less than a man" (p. 33). Van Doren then quotes with full approval Alexander Meiklejohn: "We Americans are determined that there shall not be in our society two kinds of people. We will not have two kinds of schools—one for gentlemen and ladies, the other for workers and servants. We believe that every man and woman should be a 'worker'. We believe that every man should be 'cultivated'. We believe that all men and women should govern. We believe that all men and women should be governed. All the members of our society must have both liberal and vocational education" (Van Doren, 1959; p. 32).

In *Values, Liberal Education, and National Destiny*, Earl McGrath (n.d.) tackled the same question and concluded on the basis of the research of Bloom, Block, and Carroll and others that individual differences in the seeming ability to learn are actually differences in the time required to learn: "Students below the top levels of achievement on scholastic aptitude test scores, when taught properly and given adequate time to learn, can rise to high levels of academic achievement" (pp. 45–46). This same point of view was supported in an interesting article by Jerome Kagan, who declared that the failure of some children to read, write, and add is "motiva-tional as well as intellectual and can be overcome if we change our standard pedagogical techniques" (Kaplan, 1980, p. 125).

Max Lerner (1976, p. 119) in *Values in Education* dealt with the question in this way: "In every educational system the question of *elite* and *demos* is a plaguing one: shall the major thrust of the system be toward the select (or elect—that is to say, elite) or the demos, the people? In past societies few would dare say it was any-thing but the latter. The truth is—at least for modern industrial and democratic societies—that it is a mischievous and unrewarding question. A better one to ask is how we can best make a synthesis of both aims by a values dialogue between the best of both groups."

Finally, note John Gardner's view of the matter in his book *Morale*: "Quite aside from the moral argument for opportunity, no modern nation can afford to lose the human talent that is so often buried under layers of economic and class discrimination. Modern societies run on talent, yet it's doubtful that any society has ever used more than a fraction of the talent available to it. The rest is blocked by poverty, ignorance, class barriers, prejudice, physical and mental ill health, and so on. The society must address itself to the removal of the obstacles to growth and fulfillment, whether they stem from imperfections in the society (economic deprivation, race prejudice), in the educational system (poor teaching, inadequate schools), or in the individual (sensory handicaps, mental retardation, emotional disorders)" (1978, p. 74).

As Hutchins pointed out, the issue is one of technique. How can the educational system (including not only schools and colleges but also all other educational resources) be mobilized and operated so that over several generations America might reclaim its buried talent?

Before we leave the subject of educability, note that the elementary and secondary schools are in partnership with higher education in the production of educated people. The goal of widespread education cannot be reached by higher education alone. The elementary and secondary schools have an important role not only in preparing students for college but also in educating students who may never attend college. Part of the goal of a nation of educated people is to bring the vast majority of people up to the level of high school graduate. At present, the opinion is widespread that the schools, especially the secondary schools, are not performing well their part of the educational task. To the extent that this opinion is valid, the cause of the problem is complex. (For a more detailed discussion of educability, see Bowen, 1977, chap. 11.) Technical help and moral support of the colleges and universities are needed to restore secondary education to its rightful place in the educational process.

What Would a Nation of Educated People Be Like?

How would the United States be different if as many as half or more of the adult population were well educated? There is no experience—anywhere in the world or at any time in history—to judge the consequences. We can only draw on our imagination—recognizing that any extrapolation from the effects of education for the few may not hold when education is extended to the many. As H. G. Wells (1925, p. 1304) wrote:

> But one of the hardest, most impossible tasks a writer can set himself is to picture the life of people better educated, happier in their circumstances, more free and more healthy than he is himself. We know enough today to know that there is infinite room for betterment in every human concern. Nothing is needed but collective effort. Our poverty, our restraints, our infections and indigestions, our quarrels and misunderstandings, are all things controllable and removable by concerted human action, but we know as little how life would feel without them as some poor dirty, ill-treated, fierce-souled creature born and bred amidst the cruel and dingy surroundngs of a European back street can know what it is to bathe every day, always to be clad beautifully, to climb mountains for pleasure, to fly, to meet none but agreeable, well-mannered people, to conduct researches, or make delightful things. Yet a time when all such good things will be for all men may be coming more nearly than we think. Each one who believes that brings the good time nearer; each heart that fails delays it.

We know that in our own era life in many ways is more humane, more secure, and more abundant than it was in the Middle Ages, in the nineteenth century, or even in 1950 (as shown in Chapters Three and Four), and we recognize that some of the progress we sense has been due to education. Yet we know enough about the human condition to be sure that a nation of educated people would fall short of heaven on earth. The achievement of any one goal always gives rise to new problems and objectives. There is no end to human striving and discontent. Despite the spread of education, our time has been one of great turbulence, unfulfilled expectations, and unsolved problems. So, we may ask, why push ahead toward expanded higher education when we suspect that it will not usher in the millenium?

One reason is that, like Mt. Everest, it is there. A nation of educated people is a peak to which human beings have never ascended, a planet they have never explored. Another reason is the moral precept with which this chapter opened, namely, that each person has the right, and the obligation, to achieve the highest personal development of which he is capable. Higher education is an effective instrument of personal development, and it must be made available as far as possible to all persons. Most people believe also that it is good for human life to be made more humane, more secure, and more abundant—even if these achievements do not allay all human strivings, settle all unrest, or solve all problems.

Although past experience suggests that the extension of higher education may be expected to yield important social benefits, we cannot be certain of all the consequences, positive and negative. Yet the probabilities are high that a nation that had diffused higher education to the outer limits could achieve unprecedented richness of individual human experience and surpassing cultural achievements. It would, above all, be able to draw upon virtually all rather than only part of its talent. The "mute inglorious Miltons" would shine forth. The kind of education proposed would improve communication and cohesion within the society partly by creating a vast body of persons with verbal and mathematical competence, and partly by providing a common foundation of knowledge, principles, and understandings on which to base human discourse (Boyer and Levine, 1981). Such education might also contribute to refinement of taste, manner, and conduct and possibly to a more gracious style of life.

The literature on the outcomes of higher education tells us that one of the most definite and important results of higher education, a result that differentiates educated from uneducated persons, is *the free mind*. This outcome implies freedom from prejudice, openness to new ideas, acceptance of change, and tolerance of persons of differing ideologies, cultures, and races. It is favorable to historical and geographical prespective, appreciation of different cultures, a cosmopolitan outlook, and international understanding. It encourages individuality—as distinct from conformity—among persons. It leads to wide and rapid diffusion of new ideas and new technologies. And it is conducive to social change.

If higher education exerted only the centrifugal force of the free mind, it might cause society to fly apart. But higher education also provides a centripetal counterforce by grounding human attitudes and values in the basic principles and understandings contained in the cultural heritage. The heritage is, to be sure, subject to continual study and reinterpretation, yet it changes slowly and holds in check the irresponsible flights of the free mind.

An essential element of the cultural heritage is that it radiates humane values. These call upon each person to be concerned and responsible for his fellow human beings and to be a conscientious seeker of general human betterment. The humane values include the concept that all human beings are ultimately of equal value. They also include the concept of *vocation*, namely that each person is "called" to particular occupations on the basis of service to others rather than personal gain. Still another implication of the humane values is that people of one generation have responsibility toward the people of future generations and are responsible as stewards for both the cultural heritage and the physical environment and are obliged to pass these along, not only unimpaired but improved, for the benefit of future generations. These are the kinds of values that might be disseminated from the extension of education to large numbers.

The diffusion of higher education might result in excellence in the arts and literature. It would uncover new talent and would increase appreciation and understanding of the arts and thus increase the demand for them.

In practical affairs, the spread of education would lead to improvements of health and would help people to cope with the problems of everyday living. It would reduce dependency. Perhaps its most important effect would be to improve the rearing of children, which in turn would tend over time to increase the proportion of the population prepared and motivated for higher education.

Another outcome would be the improvement of citizenship and through that of democratic government. The populace would have a deeper concern for social issues and would be more inclined to see them from a broad social and even global, rather than narrowly selfish, point of view. People would have a deeper understanding of social problems and issues, would approach them more thoughtfully, and would grasp their complexity and interrelatedness. They would participate more fully not only in voting but also in discussion and would be able to hold government more responsible and accountable. Also, by no means least, the calibre of public servants would be improved.

Finally, the diffusion of higher education would have effects on the economy. I left this point to the last because it so dominates the discussion of higher education that other equally or more important outcomes tend to be overlooked. The spread of education would be favorable in several ways to improved economic productivity. It would facilitate the discovery and training of talented entrepreneurs, managers, applied scientists, engineers, and skilled workers. It would increase the efficiency of the labor force generally by enhancing useful knowledge, personal responsibility, and health. In addition, the spread of education would facilitate the adoption of ever more advanced technologies—not only mechanical technologies but also technologies connected with the professions and the operation of social institutions such as government or education. It would contribute to the discovery of such new technologies, it would speed up the communication of novel ways of doing things, and it would increase the receptiveness of people to these new technologies.

Having described some of the major outcomes to be expected from the diffusion of education, I must concede that these results are by no means certain. In general, these are the results of education as we know it. They are at least partially documented and are widely believed. But our experience with higher education so far pertains only to a small minority of the population. Might there be a fallacy of composition in projecting the same results to the education of a majority of the population? One can imagine, for example, that an educated society would lose the work ethic, that it would become effete or decadent, that it would not be able to hold its own in international competition. Moreover, the people in an educated society might become more keenly competitive, more status conscious, more aggressive. Democratic government might be stymied when the great majority of the people were informed of their interests and aware of how to work the levers of influence in the political arena. Education might serve nefarious interests as well as benevolent purposes. These are not idle speculations. If the United States were to follow through toward a goal of a nation of educated people, it would need to fend off these negative possibilities by designing the education to produce people of toughness and energy tempered by morality and social responsibility. Education that would encourage people to become more narcissistic and self-indulgent or that would help them become more ruthless and self-seeking—that is to say, education without the balance wheel of morality and social responsibility—would be no better than ignorance.

In truth, we do not know the consequences of deepened and widened education. It is a venture just begun. It would take several generations—perhaps a century or more—to discover the ultimate outcomes. The evidence to date suggests that the nation should push on toward the goal of a nation of educated people. But this opinion is based on no more than faith that the all-round development of individual human beings will produce both individual and social benefits and that little good ultimately will come out of keeping people ignorant and excluding them from the upper reaches of culture. We can be certain that education will not bring heaven on earth. It will not obliterate all aggression, selfishness, conflict, sloth, or effeteness. But it could help make life more humane and more abundant or at least help to keep it from becoming grossly uncivilized. Winston Churchill was once asked during the course of World War II, "Why are we fighting this war?" His answer: "If we stopped, you would know why."

Agenda for Higher Education

8

I am more of a stoic about the world and thus skeptical about perfection, about the existence of "eternal spring," either in the past or in the future, but not skeptical about constant efforts at betterment of the always imperfect present.

—Clark Kerr (1977, p. 5)

To consider the responsibilities of American higher education in meeting the long-range agenda of the nation, this book began with three questions: What kind of people do we want our children and grandchildren to be? What kind of society do we want them to live in? How may education—especially higher education—be guided and shaped to help nurture people of this kind and to help create this kind of society? The time has come to draw together the various parts of the argument and to define the major tasks of American higher education not only for the decades just ahead but also for much of the twenty-first century.

Colleges and universities should, of course, continue to carry on their accustomed functions. They would educate a substantial fraction of each population cohort, they would conduct a large part of the nation's basic scientific research and much applied research, they would serve as the basic institutions for preservation and interpretation of the cultural heritage, they would continue to be major patrons of the arts, they would conduct policy analysis and would maintain a corps of experts available to serve society in many ways as needed, they would be centers of philosophical and religious inquiry, and they would engage in diverse public services (Bowen,

1977, chap. 10). Indirectly through training, research, and public service they would contribute toward economic prosperity and efficiency as they have in the past. It is to be hoped that all these functions—which may be regarded as business as usual—would be carried on with increasing effectiveness. There is urgent need, after the many years of preoccupation with growth, for increasing attention to qualitative improvement.

From the argument of the preceding chapters of this book, however, four special tasks for American higher education—beyond business as usual—were singled out: (1) to push on toward the long-range goal of *a nation of educated people*, (2) to increase the emphasis on *values* as part of the outcomes of higher education, (3) to confront the special and acute problems of *youth* in our society, and (4) to contribute toward that most compelling goal of all, *international reconciliation*. These four tasks will be considered in this final chapter.

A Nation of Educated People

The ideal of a nation of educated people was described in some detail in Chapter Seven. It refers to the eventual extension of higher learning to a large portion of the entire population. The process should occur as rapidly as possible, but its full attainment would probably require several generations. The concept of "a nation of educated people" was advocated primarily on moral grounds—as an eventuality that would be desirable for its own sake without regard for ulterior consequences. But it would likely also produce valuable side effects for the democracy, the economy, and the culture.

During the past several decades, the United States has pursued this goal energetically. Higher educational enrollments have grown from 2 million in 1946 to 12 million in 1980. Today, nearly half of each age cohort of the population at least enter college and more than a quarter receive baccalaureates. Even in the decade of the 1970s, which was supposed to have been a sluggish and depressed period for higher education, enrollments increased by over 40 percent. Through generous student aid, open-ended admissions, and remedial programs, higher education can reach an ever-increasing proportion of the people.

As the expansion has continued, however, growing pains have emerged. The ability level of students as measured by test scores has declined. Many students come to college with inadequate secondary preparation—especially in verbal and mathematical skills. Many attend part-time and live off-campus, thus dividing their attention between education, jobs, families, and off-campus recreation. Such part-time nonresident students often do not have access to full-time professors, laboratories, libraries, counselors, and the cultural and social opportunities of the campus. They do not receive the total immersion in higher education that is experienced by traditional students who attend full-time and in residence. Furthermore, the current generation of students is strongly motivated toward vocational education and their receptivity to personal or liberal learning is less than that of their predecessors of a few decades ago.

These problems suggest to some that the nation is approaching a limit to its ability to extend higher education to ever-increasing numbers. I am inclined to agree with this assessment, but I would regard the limit as a temporary barrier to be overcome rather than as a permanent restriction to be passively accepted. But the situation does suggest that the higher educational community should be giving greater attention to quality as it continues to extend quantity—perhaps at a slower rate.

American colleges and universities have taken on a tremendous load of new students over a relatively brief period. A pause may help educators learn to cope with the problems involved in serving these new students before resuming growth of numbers. Many things should be done, among them:

- Work with elementary and secondary schools in improving preparation for college
- Encourage more students to attend full-time in residence at least for part of their college careers and thus to partake more fully of the facilities and opportunities of campus life
- Find new ways of enriching the social and cultural experiences of part-time and commuter students, perhaps through creation of neighborhood centers or through use of facilities of the wider community, such as museums, libraries, symphony orchestras, churches, botanical gardens, and other cultural amenities

- Bring about a better balance and harmonization of vocational and liberal education
- Enhance the personalization of the many campuses that have become outsize during the era of growth

Indeed, a decline in enrollment due to demographic changes would be most welcome if the higher educational community could apply the resources thus liberated to the enormous task of improving quality; then the stage could be set for the next wave of growth.

Despite the desirability of breathing space to give attention to quality, the fact remains that millions of people in the United States who are not now participating in higher education are possible candidates for further education. Consider, for example, the substantial numbers of youth who are unprepared for college not because of inherent personal limitations but because of social disadvantages, tardy maturation, inadequate information or guidance, or lack of incentives. Consider that the percentage of each cohort attending college is half in some states what it is in others. Consider the large numbers of youth who would be qualified to graduate from college but drop out or fail to transfer from two-year to four-year institutions (Breneman, 1981). If all the youth who actually are qualified for college—or under different circumstances could become qualified—were to attend, enrollments would be increased by several millions.

Consider also that nearly three quarters of all adults (twenty-five and over) have never been to college. These potential learners are of special importance. If they could be educated in large numbers, the time required to achieve a nation of educated people would be greatly shortened (Watkins, 1980). When formal education is confined to youth, the educated adult population grows only by the annual additions of young people and self-educated adults. The number of these people is small relative to the total adult population, and so the well-educated as a percentage of all adults grows only gradually. For example, at the present rate of college graduation among the youthful cohorts, which is about 28 percent, it would take fifty to sixty years to bring the educated adult population up to 28 percent. With the constant addition to the population of immigrants, most of whom are not well educated, the time required would be even longer.

The task of the higher educational community is to bring both youthful and adult learners into the mainstream of American society, and thus to speed up the process of extending education and at the same time of salvaging vast amounts of neglected talent. The number of people who have not graduated from college, including both youth and adults, is of the order of 100 million. Small additions to the percentage attending college would make substantial differences in enrollments. Every 1 percent would add a million students. If adult learning is to have its full impact, however, it should reach out to persons of limited education. Adult learning as it has evolved in recent years has been predominantly a preserve of the already well-educated. Participation rates have been highly correlated with previous education. This participation is logical: People who are already educated have the necessary resources, confidence in their own ability, and understanding of the value of education—qualities that persons with meagre education often lack.

I do not hold that in the near future a majority of the people could become well educated in the sense in which I have defined that term. But it is likely, over the next several generations, that the barriers of limited cultural background, deplorable schooling, inadequate financial means, and weak incentives could be surmounted to the extent that at least half of the people could become well educated. It is an obligation of the nation and of the higher educational system to salvage the vast amounts of wasted potential ability, without neglecting the discovery and nurturing of exceptional talent.

Though some relief from the provision for numbers—some breathing space—may be needed in the coming years in the interests of quality, the higher educational system should not lose its sense of urgency or its momentum. It would be tragic if decades were to pass without progress in both numbers of students and quality of education. For this progress to occur, vigorous efforts are needed to extend higher education to both youthful and adult learners. These efforts should include the preparation of people with inadequate secondary education and the discovery through inquiry and experimentation of the pedagogical techniques and practical arrangements necessary to bring effective higher education to new categories of students. As Peter Drucker has written (forthcoming):

The greatest challenge to educators is likely to come from our new opportunities for diversity. We now have the chance to apply the basic findings of psychological, developmental, and educational research over the last 100 years: namely that no one educational method fits all children.

Almost all youngsters—and apparently "oldsters" as well—are capable of attaining the same standards within a reasonable period of time. All but a few babies, for instance, learn to walk by the age of two and to talk by the age of three. But no two get there quite the same way, as parents have known for eons.

So too at higher levels. Some children learn best by rote, in structured environments with high certainty and strict discipline. Others thrive in the less structured "permissive" atmosphere of a "progressive" school. Some adults learn out of books, some learn by doing, some learn best by listening. Some students need prescribed daily doses of information; others need challenge, the "broad picture," and a high degree of responsibility for the design of their own work. But for too long, educators have insisted that there is one best way to teach and learn, even though they have disagreed about what that way is.

Education for Values

For thousands of years, educational philosophers in the Western tradition have advocated an education designed for the unfolding of the student's whole personality. They have advocated not only the learning of substantive knowledge and the cultivation of physical proficiency but also, above all, the acquisition of sound values. In this context, values refer to standards of choice that individuals not only understand intellectually but also internalize as a basis of actual conduct. These standards of choice are related to many aspects of human life, for example, family relations, political affairs, work, intellectual activities, interpersonal relations, religious experience, esthetic matters, and recreation. Values as so defined are hierarchical. Some carry greater weight than others, and those to which the greatest weight and corresponding sanctions are attached are called *moral values*. For example, if a person prefers modern to Renaissance art or advocates the income tax instead of the sales tax, these are matters of value but not necessarily of morality. But if a scientist falsifies data or a business disposes of toxic wastes in an unsafe manner or parents neglect their children, these are matters of morality (Morrill, 1980, pp. 62-67, 71).

As indicated in Chapter Five, a free society characterized by a democratic government and a capitalistic economy is only as good as the values the people bring to it. The government and the economy will respond to whatever values the people seek through their votes and their cash outlays. A nation, therefore, depends on the various institutions of education—especially the family, church, school, college, and media—to transmit worthy values to the people who in turn will guide the government and the economy toward the conditions of a good society. These same worthy values are also the foundation on which individual persons can build good lives. The distinguishing feature—the foundation—of a good society and a free society, then, is a people with a coherent system of sound moral values, including especially social responsibility, sense of vocation, loyalty to the truth, humane sensibilities, and parental obligations. And the distinguishing feature of a great civilization is a people having sound values and therefore capable of sound choices in the realms of ideas, manners, personal consumption, esthetics, health and physical skill, recreation, and other aspects of what is today glibly called "life-style." Without such a foundation, neither a free society nor a good society is possible. No amount of education directed exclusively toward positive knowledge and technical skill can produce a great civilization. Such education may work technological wonders, but it will merely intensify the grasping, the conniving, the fierce rivalries, and the disorders that always lurk near the surface of all human societies. Such education must be leavened with sound values, or it will end in catastrophe rather than richly civilized life.

As indicated in Chapters Three and Four, the principal problems confronting America today are rooted in the inadequacy of our prevailing values, especially in a weakness of our sense of social responsibility. This inadequacy is plainly exposed as the nation struggles with the economic problems of inflation, unemployment, environmental deterioration, and depletion of natural resources. It is present in connection with the social problems of crime, drug abuse, and alcoholism. It is particularly evident in the deficiencies of the family, the schools, and the mass media. And it is apparent in connection with the problems of pressure-group democracy and, on an international scale, with the constant threat of war. Perhaps the most important function of higher education as related to the agenda of the nation is to educate people with values and perspectives such that they will be aware of, and act upon, their social responsibilities.

In the solution of most of the problems I have cited, techniques as well as values are involved. Higher education, of course, has a responsibility through its teaching, research, and public service to produce and disseminate necessary technical knowledge and skills. But knowledge and skills will be of little avail without the inclination to tackle the problems with the general public interest at heart, and this motivation can arise only with a responsible and caring leadership supported by a responsible and caring public.

If social responsibility is accepted as crucial, what can the American higher educational community do to raise the quality of the values that prevail in our society? I must concede that this question is not easy to answer. There are no standard and time-tested recipes waiting to be adopted. The literature on educational outcomes suggests that higher education does in fact influence moderately the values of its students and that the effects are on the whole consistent with widely accepted goals of education (Bowen, 1977; Hyman, 1979). Indeed, common sense suggests that an experience as lengthy and profound as several years of college education is bound to have some influence on values—whether or not that influence is intended. And from that obvious fact, one may draw the inference that educators had better be concerned about the kind of influence they are exerting and about the kind of influence they ought to be exerting. Neglect of values may be one way of influencing them. It may be a signal that values are unimportant. Clearly, there is need for inquiry into and discussion of ways and means and of practical experimentation. The time is propitious. There is growing interest in values not only in many liberal arts colleges where curricula are now under scrutiny but also in professional schools where faculties are wrestling with the problem of how to produce socially responsible physicians, lawyers, engineers, business leaders, and other professionals. And there is a growing body of sophisticated literature on education for values.

Despite the need for greater attention to values and the signs of increasing interest, four cautionary comments are in order. First, the academic community is not of a single mind either on the possibility of affecting values through higher education or on the desirability of including the transmittal of values among the objectives of our colleges and universities. Many academic people are engrossed in their technical specialties and scholarly endeavors and do not acknowledge responsibility for the values acquired by their students. Second, it is generally agreed that there are severe limitations on the amount of influence colleges and universities can expect to exert on the values of students—even with the best of intentions and the best of techniques. The college experience is only one of many influences on values, and it occurs at a time in students' lives when their values have already been largely, and to some extent irrevocably, formed. Third, even when practicing educators wish to do something about values, knowledge of how to proceed is precarious. Fourth, most of the obvious techniques for education in values are of doubtful efficacy. One of these methods is exhortation, a form of which is crude indoctrination; another is the objective study or analysis of values. Neither of these techniques appears to result in the internalization of values. Merely knowing the good deed is not readily transformed into doing the good deed. Apparently, subtler techniques are more useful, for example, encouraging free discussion of issues, dilemmas, and alternatives, or putting students into contact with appropriate mentors, or providing an environment that is supportive of sound ethical and esthetic values.

Any college or university that attempts to influence the values of its students will do well to heed these disclaimers. Nevertheless, the task is eminently worth attempting, and it is of vital importance to the society that it be attempted. In the remainder of this section, I shall suggest some practical approaches to the transmission of sound values through higher education.

The Curriculum. Much of the past discussion of values education has long been centered on the curriculum. The assumption has been that the choice of subjects taught, the degree requirements, and the advice given students about choice of courses will affect the kinds of values students will acquire. The most widely accepted article of faith has been that a liberal education, especially one in which the humanities have a prominent place, will be favorable to the transmission of good values. Obversely, vocational or technical curricula have been suspected of having negligible or even adverse influences. In any event, as faculties have considered education for values, their attention has been focused primarily on the course requirements of the liberal arts curriculum. Actual knowledge of the relationship between the curriculum and the values acquired by students is almost nonexistent. Furthermore, many faculty debates on curricula turn out to be political contests relating to the interests of competing departments rather than serious consideration of educational issues. Nevertheless, common sense would suggest that a curriculum ought to contain a generous representation of subjects in which important value questions arise naturally and in which there is a tradition of concern for values.

In Chapter Seven, I attempted to define the characteristics of the "well-educated person." As part of this definition, I presented an "ideal" curriculum covering the last two years of high school and four years of college. This proposed curriculum, though quite conventional, included many subjects that are heavily laden with values, among them, history of Western civilization, philosophy, religious studies, geography, career opportunities, humanities, arts, social studies, and even natural science. The proposed curriculum would provide ample opportunity for involving students with values in a wide variety of settings and circumstances. In Chapter Seven, the "well-educated" person was defined also in terms of a set of attributes he or she would possess. These would include loyalty to the truth, the free mind, historic perspective, cosmopolitan outlook, sense of vocation, social responsibility, concern for human equality, love of learning, and other similar qualities. The pedagogical problem is to use the curriculum to instill these desired personal attributes. This transition, however, is anything but automatic. A well-designed curriculum only provides opportunities for values education—abundant opportunities but no guarantees. There is more to values education than selecting the right list of courses. What happens depends greatly on the content of the courses.

Course Content. Every course, no matter how factual or technical the subject, may be taught in a way that impinges on values. At the very minimum, any course may influence, either positively or negatively, such values as respect for the truth, thoroughness, and self-discipline. And in most courses, a broader range of value questions are readily present and can be naturally brought to the surface. For example, a subject as technical as chemistry raises value questions relating to health, safety, environmental protection, and esthetics; similarly, accounting raises innumerable value questions relating to personal and corporate integrity. Indeed, some of the most promising values education is occurring today in a few professional schools. At the same time, any course, no matter how laden with values, can be taught in a way that emphasizes factual knowledge and technique and plays down value questions. Sadly, even the most humanistic subjects such as literature, philosophy, religion, or history can be taught in ways that ignore questions of value.

Values do not respect the conventional classifications of subjects. Many faculties go astray by assuming that an appropriate list of course requirements is all that is needed for education. The debate ends when the course offerings and course requirements are established. But in truth, these are only the beginning.

All subjects—from the most prosaic and technical to the most humanistic or transcendental—involve positive knowledge relating to fact and technique, as well as standards of choice relating to personal morals, public policy, esthetic judgments, and other value questions. What is needed in all education is a balance between factual-technical learning and values education. As indicated in the preceding section, this balance may be reached partly by the design of the curriculum and the advising of students, which together regulate the mixture of subjects to be studied as between those that emphasize fact and technique and those that give prominence to questions of value. But the design of the curriculum does not achieve the desired result unless the courses offered are actually taught in ways that balance the two modes of learning.

There are many ways to introduce value questions into ordinary courses—for example, through comparative study of different cultures or of different historical eras; through reference to pertinent biographical or autobiographical literature, drama, novels, poetry, and case materials; and through study of actual issues in international relations, environmental protection, human rights, public regulation, and social responsibility. In some situations, role playing, simulation techniques, and games may be useful. Course content may be enriched by interplay between the abstract and the concrete, theory and practice, and reflection and experience. Throughout, there is need to combine and reconcile liberal and vocational education by introducing a liberal dimension into vocational subjects and a practical dimension into liberal subjects. Perhaps most important of all, students should be challenged at various times and in various ways to consider such questions as: "Who am I?" "What is the good life?" "What kind of person do I want to become?" If questions of value appear at many points in the academic careers of students, these values will tend to provide a common element to the educational experience of all students. They will help to lend coherence to the curriculum and overcome the fragmentation and disconnectedness that is the bane of contemporary higher education.

The Faculty. Values education depends not alone on what is taught and the way it is taught but also on the kind of people who are doing the teaching. Faculty are in many cases influential in shaping the values of students. By this I do not mean that students invariably adopt the values exhibited by faculty. They may sometimes be repelled by the faculty's values. I also do not mean that students are influenced by every faculty member they encounter. Sometimes only a few or even a single teacher may become a model or mentor who exerts decisive influence on a student. And faculty influence is not always favorable; it may be quite the opposite. But there can be little doubt that faculty do influence student values, for better or for worse and that the kind of people who make up the faculty affects the kind of people students become. As Miller and Orr (1980, p. 14) have written, "It is not only in systematic ethical argument, political addresses, and sermons that moral images are enunciated. Moral images are also manifested in the lives of individuals who populate communities, whether religious or academic."

The values of most faculty members are strongly oriented toward technical competence and scholarly achievement in a relatively narrow subspecialty. Their training and the criteria for their appointment, promotion, and professional recognition place great emphasis on research or scholarship in a chosen field and on the communication of this subject matter to professional peers and to students. In their teaching, most faculty feel responsible mainly for the progress of their students in a particular subject and for transmitting the scholarly virtues related to technical competence in that field. They seldom feel responsible for the development of their students as whole persons. Moreover, many faculty are not well informed about the process of human development and are not skilled in aspects of pedagogy that go beyond the transmittal of knowledge within narrow special fields. Under these conditions, values education tends to be confined to matters of technical competence. However, some faculty members rise above technique. Some convey the relationships of their specialties to the broader range of knowledge, some bring out the value questions that flow from their subjects, some convey love of learning and passion for the truth, some take an interest in the all-round personal development of their students. Through the selection of faculty and a reward system that encourages attention to values, colleges and universities could enrich their influence or values.

Campus Environment. A traditional and influential instrument of values education is the general atmosphere and surroundings of student life. In an earlier day when most students attended full-time and lived on or near their campuses and when the rule of *in loco parentis* prevailed, the general campus environment was usually regarded as a powerful influence—both positive and negative. Today, it is probably somewhat less potent for the large minority of full-time residental students and considerably less influential for those who attend part time and live away from campus. Nevertheless, for most students, the general campus environment is a significant influence, especially in the realm of values—partly for what it offers and partly for what it lacks. Institutions differ greatly in the character of the environment they provide and probably have correspondingly different impacts on the values of students.

The environment consists in part of the physical features of the campus—the layout and design of the buildings, the grounds, and the traffic patterns. Values are clearly expressed through design and maintenance. They are expressed also in the relative importance assigned to various facilities such as chapels, museums, theatres, playing fields, gymnasiums, and stadiums.

The environment includes also the prevailing patterns of extracurricular life in the institution. It is made up of a host of facilities and activities, among them, housing and dining arrangements, recreational activities, sports, and cultural activities in fields such as religion, music, art, theatre, literature, debate, journalism, and public affairs. And it includes prevailing attitudes of the campus community such as democratic spirit, liberal political views, religious interest, internationalism, altruism, or friendliness.

Still other features of the environment are the basic values underlying the decisions and actions of the faculty and administration of the institution. To what extent do they espouse the traditional ethos of colleges and universities, which includes such values as adherence to the truth, freedom of the mind, cosmopolitan outlook, historic perspective, cultivation of the arts, human equality, social responsibility, and sense of vocation? To what extent do they engage in corrupt athletic practices or tolerate shoddy academic standards? How amenable are they to altering institutional missions in order to attract and retain students? To what extent do they embrace bureaucratic methods of administration at the sacrifice of concern for students as individuals? To what extent is decision making closed and arbitrary rather than open and participatory? On the other hand, to what extent are administrative decisions consistent and equitable? The style of administration in a college or university radiates many signals to students about the kinds of values that are deemed acceptable by the leadership of the institution. Administrative behavior that seems inconsistent with traditional academic values may undermine values education.

A fourth feature of the college environment, one that exerts a powerful influence over each student, is the student peer group. The characteristics of the peer group—including the values they embrace—are determined partly by the collegiate environment. But they are determined too by the traits the students bring with them when they come to college. These traits are determined in part by social class, family backgrounds, and previous educational experiences. Some institutions are able to control the composition of the peer groups through their admission process and thus exert some control over the influence of the peer group. Other institutions, even though nonselective, consistently attract students from particular social groups, for example, given ethnic or religious or income classes. In such institutions the peer group tends to be fairly stable. Some institutions, however, particularly those whose educational mission is changing or whose market area is subject to major shifts in population, sometimes find themselves with greatly altered student bodies and peer groups. But in all cases, the body of peers is a potent influence on each student individually, one that can never be wholly controlled by a college or university.

Finally, the overall environments of individual colleges and universities contain the traditions that are handed down from generation to generation. These traditions retard the rate of change in the environments and lend continuity to the concern for values.

Institutional environments convey values more or less spontaneously. They send signals to students—sometimes very subtle signals—about the values that are acceptable, tolerated, or discouraged. Environments also provide many experiences—in the concert hall, museum, chapel, playing field, or residence hall—that help to form values. The environment has the advantage that most parts of it are optional. It does not overtly preach or teach and is flexible enough to allow a range of behavior. But it is always there, exerting a quiet but persistent and, in the long run, effective influence on the way people think and believe and behave not only in their student days but throughout their lives.

It is a pity that college environments have in recent decades become less effective in the sense that millions of students, the part-time commuters, cannot partake of them as fully as full-time residential students. To carry out its responsibility in the formation of values, one of the key tasks before higher education is to find ways of bringing more students to the campus as full-time residents or, when this is not possible, of finding substitutes for full-time campus residence. The traditional residential college or university was an elite institution and bears some of the opprobrium attached to elitism. The ideal to be sought is to bring to large numbers of people the ambience of the residential campus or the best possible substitutes.

Private Institutions. A comment is in order about the role of private colleges and universities in the advancement of liberal learning. On the whole, but with many exceptions, private institutions have probably been more attentive to values education than public institutions. The comparative success of the private institutions may have been due in part to smaller enrollments, which have enabled them to provide personalized education. It may also stem from their greater dedication to the liberal tradition and, in some cases, it may be attributed to religious ties. Though the pressure on many private institutions to bow to the demands of students for vocational training has been almost overwhelming, the great private universities, the stronger liberal arts colleges, and many church-related institutions have been able to resist these pressures and to persevere in offering traditional liberal education. These institutions, by serving as living examples, have helped all of higher education to keep alive the ideal of education for values. I am not suggesting that all private colleges are models of liberal learning or that all public institutions have sold out to crass vocationalism. But by serving as visible and influential examples of values education, many private institutions have helped shape the prevailing popular concept of what a college or university should be like, and they have thus assisted the public institutions in adhering to their liberal heritage. The preservation and renewal of the private sector of higher education is therefore of utmost importance.

Literature. It would be tempting to conclude with an extended discussion of how to conduct colleges that are effective in values education. I have resisted the temptation because others, far better qualified than I, have written superb tracts and treatises on the subject. Values education has not lacked for wise and lucid expositors. Great wisdom and inspiration is to be found in the educational writings of Confucius, Plato, Aristotle, the Medieval theologians, Luther, Erasmus, Comenius, Bacon, Milton, Rousseau, Pestalozzi, Jefferson, Newman, Arnold, Mill, Emerson, Dewey, and Whitehead. All of these and many more were advocates of liberal learning and were deeply concerned with the transmittal of values. In our generation, there has been a steady flow of literature on liberal learning and values education encompassing both philosophical foundations and practical applications. This flow of literature has persisted even in the past few decades, when the liberal view of education has been on the defensive and perhaps on the wane. From this literature, I have selected sixteen books that have appealed to me as exceptionally useful:

- Robert Maynard Hutchins, *The Higher Learning in America,* 1936.
- Harvard Committee, *General Education in a Free Society,* 1945.
- Sir Walter Moberly, *The Crisis in the University,* 1949.
- Mark Van Doren, *Liberal Education,* 1959.
- Philip H. Phenix, *Education and the Common Good,* 1961.
- Daniel Bell, *The Reforming of General Education,* 1966.
- University of California, Berkeley, Academic Senate, *Education at Berkeley* (the Muscatine Report, Charles Muscatine and others), 1966.
- Carnegie Commission on Higher Education, *The Purposes and the Performance of Higher Education in the U. S. Approaching the Year 2000,* 1973.
- Earl F. Cheit, *The Useful Arts and the Liberal Tradition,* 1975.
- Max Lerner, *Values in Education,* 1976.
- Earl J. McGrath, *General Education and the Plight of Modern Man,* n.d. (c. 1975).
- Eva T. H. Brann, *Paradoxes of Education in a Republic,* 1979.
- Martin Kaplan (Editor), *What Is an Educated Person?,* 1980.
- Richard L. Morrill, *Teaching Values in College,* 1980.
- Daniel Callahan and Sissela Bok (Editors), *Ethics Teaching in Higher Education,* 1980.
- Ernest Boyer and Arthur Levine, *A Quest for Common Learning,* 1981.

These books are brief, highly literate, and stimulating. They could all be read in the course of a two weeks' holiday. But if time presses and only a few can be read, I recommend Hutchins, Phenix, Lerner, Boyer and Levine, and especially Morrill. I single out Morrill because his book combines philosophy and practice in a most artful way. Another fruitful source of ideas and practical knowledge is the many publications of the Association of American Colleges. This organization has concentrated its entire program and all its resources on the study and advancement of liberal education.

American Youth

In my review of social trends presented in Chapters Three and Four, I found that the period since World War II has in many respects been a time of substantial and sustained progress. The standard of living rose spectacularly, 40 million new jobs were created, health and longevity were improved, the resources devoted to human welfare and education were expanded at an unprecedented rate, the arts and sciences flourished, a significant beginning was made in environmental protection and resource conservation, and progress was achieved in human rights, equality, and freedom. During this same period, however, certain grave and intractable problems emerged—stubborn inflation and the growing threat of war being the most notorious. But there was also a cluster of interrelated problems that affect human welfare adversely. These included the weakening and instability of the family, the decline of the schools and neighborhoods, the increasingly deleterious influence of the media of mass communications, the spread of crime, the unprecedented use of drugs, rising alcoholism, and persistent unemployment. These problems affect people of all ages and classes, but they bear down with special severity on youth. Together, they represent what can only be described as the gross neglect of youth in contemporary society.

I hasten to qualify the blanket indictment of the family, the schools, and the media. There are, of course, millions of strong families, many excellent schools, and worthy media. Yet, there has been widespread and serious deterioration of these institutions that are so critically important in the development of youth. The nation has slipped into an unsatisfactory pattern in the rearing of its children. The neglect is so evident and widespread as to suggest that children in our society are no longer loved. Millions of children are in broken homes and many more in homes of working parents where supervision and guidance is wanting. Increasing numbers come from homes where they are in one way or another neglected and some are even abused. Many go to schools that do not teach. Millions of children spend hours with the communications media, both printed and electronic, that at best stupefy and at worst disseminate violence, pornography, and vulgar material values. Many are relegated to unwholesome neighborhoods. The results of these conditions are ignorance, illiteracy, distorted values, illegitimacy, crime and delinquency, drug abuse, unemployment, mental illness, alienation, and a perpetuation of these same conditions in succeeding generations.

These conditions are not peculiar to the United States. They exist, more or less, in most industrial and urban societies throughout the world. The late twentieth century is not the golden age of youth anywhere. The problem seems to be of greatest severity in the adolescent years among disadvantaged youth who are or should be making the transition from school to work. For those young people who continue in high school to graduation, go on to college, and then enter the labor force, a relatively smooth transition from school to work under institutional guidance and protection is provided. But for those who try to move directly from high school to jobs, especially if they are high school dropouts, the transition from school to work is fraught with uncertainty. Both institutional and parental support are at a minimum (Carnegie Council on Policy Studies in Higher Education, 1980). Unfortunately, the children have no lobby.

The Carnegie Council on Policy Studies in Higher Education (1980, pp. 17–18) constructed an informative typology of youth as follows:

> I. *The Advantaged:* young persons from families in the top two thirds of the income range and who finish high school.
> II. *The Financially Disadvantaged:* young persons from families in the bottom one third of the income range who finish high school but, where doing so, may impose a financial hardship on their families and where attendance in college does impose such a hardship.
> III. *The Socially Deprived:* young persons who do not finish high school for reasons of social circumstances (family and community deprivations and social prejudices).
> IV. *The Personally Deprived:* young persons who do not finish high school for reasons of personal circumstances (mental, physical, or psychological disabilities).
> V. *The Opt-Outs:* young persons who do not choose to participate in established educational or economic institutions of society for reasons of personal choice or philosophical orientation.

Using this typology, the Carnegie Council estimated the distribution of youth among the several categories shown in Table 5. Nearly half of all youth (47 percent, or about 12 million young persons) are subject to some disadvantage and more than a quarter (27 percent or

Table 5. Estimated Distribution of Population Aged 16 to 21
by Carnegie Typology and by Ethnic Groups

| | All Youth | | | | |
	Percent	Number (millions)	Black	Hispanic	White
Advantaged	53%	13.3	27%	31%	59%
Financially disadvantaged	20	5.0	38	29	18
Socially deprived	18	4.5	23	32	15
Personally deprived	3	0.8	3	3	3
Opt-outs	6	1.5	9	5	5
Total	100	25.1	100	100	100

nearly 7 million) are subject to serious deprivation. If to these figures were added those youths classed as advantaged but who have significant psychological and other problems and those young people under sixteen and over twenty-one whose lives are in some way blighted, the 7 million might be raised to 10 million or more, a number nearly equal to the total enrollments in all of higher education. Some of these people doubtless overcome their early handicaps, just as some people who were not deprived in their youth turn out badly. But many of the deprived probably go through life with handicaps, much talent is lost to society as a result of their deprivation, and the costs to society in dependency, crime, mental illness, drug abuse, alcoholism, poor health, and squalor is enormous. The outlook is more disturbing when it is realized that the youthful disadvantaged are concentrated heavily among minority groups. At current and expected rates of growth, by the year 2000, minority youth will constitute 25 to 30 percent of all youth. Progress toward the general advancement of our culture, including the goal of "a nation of educated people," depends on the amelioration of these conditions through the conservation and development of our least advantaged people. The Carnegie Council (1980, p. 11) observed:

> The public attention directed at [youth] unemployment
> has obscured the many other and more serious problems. Youth
> in America is not suffering from a single malady (unemploy-

ment), and no single patent medicine (full employment) will
cure the many illnesses. We have instead a growth, more like a
cancer in our body politic—causes not fully known, cure not fully
known. But it creates great pain in the suffering of ruined lives,
crime, drug addiction, lost hopes, social fears, reduced productivity, raised social expenditures, and disdain for authority. The concentration on unemployment has largely buried from sight the
deeper problems. This has been a disservice to the American people. We face a cancer, not a common cold.

But does higher education have responsibilities relating to
the least capable and the least promising of our youth? If so, what
are these responsibilities? Historically, the posture of higher education has been to reject and ignore the less promising young people
by selecting out the more promising and concentrating its resources
on them. I do not suggest any drastic change in this historic practice. The immediate function of higher education is to serve qualified persons. But its larger function is to help increase the number
who can become qualified. Moreover, the higher educational
community and the society at large cannot ignore the glaring
inequity when more resources of money and attention are bestowed
on the young people who attend college than on those who do not.

For several reasons, the higher educational community
cannot properly be indifferent to the circumstances of any young
people. First, a primary function of colleges and universities is to
extend education to ever-increasing numbers. It cannot carry out
this function unless increasing numbers are prepared for college
through sound nurturing by families, schools, churches, media, and
other influences. Second, without adequate preparation of incom-
ing students, the academic standards of colleges and universities will
be dragged down by the inability of students to perform properly
and by the necessity of providing remedial and watered-down education. Third, the high school is a major partner of the colleges in
liberal education. The colleges cannot be self-sufficient in liberal
education and must depend on the high school for half or more of
this task. Fourth, the colleges and universities recruit and train the
teachers, counselors, and administrators for the lower schools, they
conduct the research and development related to elementary and
secondary education, and they write most of the textbooks and pre-

pare most of the other instructional materials used in the lower schools. Higher education also educates and trains the clergy, the jounalists, the social workers, the physicians, the business leaders, the military officers, and many other persons who are involved in the education and welfare of youth. Finally, fifth, colleges and universities conduct the adult education for many of those who missed out on higher education during youth. (See also President's Commission for a National Agenda for the Eighties, 1980a.)

As the locus of all these critical activities, higher education bears a heavy and inescapable responsibility for what goes on in the world of youth. The higher educational community cannot stand aloof from the youth problem of our society and claim that it is somebody else's business. It is, of course, not the exclusive responsibility of higher education, but higher education has a huge stake in it. But what can higher education do? And what should it do?

The role of the four-year colleges and universities flows directly from their primary functions in teaching, research, and public service. Like most social problems, the youth problem is interdisciplinary. Though it centers on the family, the school, and the workplace, it involves psychology, economics, sociology, politics, education, religion, social work, medicine, military science, and many other disciplines. Any college or university entering the field should organize a youth task force with the various disciplines represented and with dedicated and capable leadership. However, some institutions might prefer to concentrate their efforts in schools of education, partly because these schools are already interdisciplinary and partly because many of them have experienced declining enrollments and have resources that could be directed toward the youth problem.

The objectives of higher education would be (1) to motivate and prepare professional persons to serve effectively in capacities relating to youth institutions such as families, child care centers, schools, churches, employers, and armed services; (2) to conduct research and development relating to the youth problem, including demonstration programs and projects; (3) to conduct public service or extension programs to assist schools and other community institutions in dealing with youth problems; (4) to provide educational programs and materials useful to families, schools, neighborhood groups, child care centers, employers, and the general public; and (5) to facilitate the admission to college of disadvantaged youth by learning to provide more effective remedial programs at both the secondary and college levels. Beginnings along these lines are being made by various colleges and universities individually and collectively within the spirit of Title XI of the Education Amendments of 1980. (For an account of plans and progress among urban colleges and universities, see Mayville, 1980.)

These proposals hark back to the early days of agricultural training, research, and extension. The need for comparable programs relating to youth is no less than it was a century ago for farmers. The task is enormous and progress is bound to be slow, but it is time to get started. And the universities and colleges are among the most promising vehicles.

One proposal that at least exemplifies the need for new and radical approaches to the youth problem is to establish residential schools designed specifically for talented but disadvantaged urban youth. These institutions would encompass the last two years of high school and the first two years of college. They would be modeled somewhat on the plan of Berea College or the School of the Ozarks but would serve urban rather than predominantly rural clienteles. Such schools would be selective in admitting students, would establish high academic standards, and would emphasize work and other virtues along with study. They would offer liberal education though not necessarily to the exclusion of vocational training. They would be located in places well-removed from inner cities. Students would graduate whenever they were prepared for upper-division work in suitable colleges or universities of conventional type. Tuition, board, and room would be free except for the obligations of students to work part time. Such schools might be established and operated with public or private funding by existing colleges or universities. It is even possible that some existing colleges might find a new mission and new sources of support by shifting their role to that of residential school for talented but disadvantaged youth.

Within higher education, community colleges have become a leading presence in the youth field, and they have much to contribute. The community colleges began as general education centers for local freshman and sophomore students destined to tranfer to distant four-year colleges and universities. The mission of community colleges, however, soon began to evolve toward increasing emphasis on vocational education, on adult education, on part-time students, and on minority students. Today they have virtually become the supermarkets of higher education with highly varied students and equally varied services. These trends have gone so far that many community colleges have almost lost their original function of preparing students to transfer to the upper division of four-year institutions. Indeed, some leaders of the community college would see the future of their institutions as community learning and service centers functioning not only as higher educational institutions for conventional students but also as community centers for counseling, job placement, community planning, extension programs, youth activities and programs, and whatever else needs to be done locally toward human development (Gleazer, 1980).

The Carnegie Council on Policy Studies in their report, *Giving Youth a Better Chance* (1980, p. 25), advocated that "the community colleges should take on a residual responsibility for youth." This function would require that "they be available to all youths in the community to advise on academic and occupational opportunities, to offer job preparation classes, to make job placements, to work out individual combinations of employment and classroom instruction, to develop and to make referrals to service opportunities, to make referrals to Comprehensive Employment and Training Act (CETA) employers, to make referrals to sources of legal and medical advice, to refer to and to create apprenticeship programs. Additional and specialized personnel will be required for this purpose. These might be known as 'youth service functions.' Youths would be given an institutional base of operation. We badly need better and more encompassing 'institutions for the young.'" In considering this recommendation, David Breneman (1980) suggested that foundations or governmental agencies might appropriately provide grants to particular community colleges to initiate such "youth service functions" on an experimental basis. (See also Breneman and Nelson, 1981.)

Another approach to the youth problem would be to integrate education and work with such programs as the following:

- Work study and cooperative education available for high school as well as college students
- Facilitation of youth employment through placement services, subsidization of employers of youth, or a differential minimum wage for youth
- Community work-education councils to link education and work (Wirtz, 1975)
- Earlier and easier entry into the armed forces
- National youth service

The last of these, *national youth service,* would be a comprehensive nationwide program providing opportunities for young people to serve the nation over a period of a year or more. Many proposals along this line have been presented. Some would require compulsory service for all, some selective service, and others voluntary service. Some would require military service only and others would provide various options involving military or civilian service. These recommendations have gathered considerable support among informed specialists, the general public, and young people themselves.* Clearly the present and forseeable conjunction of youth problems and military manpower problems strongly suggest that national youth service should be carefully considered among the options available to the nation. The implications for higher education would, of course, be tremendous. Higher education might well be directly involved in national youth service, just as colleges and universities were involved in military training during World War I and II. But more important, national youth service might, in the long run, help to prepare and motivate a larger proportion of the youthful population to undertake higher education and so help in achieving the goal of a nation of educated people.

---

*Steven Muller (1978), president of Johns Hopkins University, Leon Botstein (1980), president of Bard College, and George Eppley (1981), of Cuyahoga Community College, have all become strong advocates. The Sloan Commission on Government and Higher Education produced an excellent working paper on the subject outlining the various options (White, 1978).

International Reconciliation

Throughout this volume, I have repeatedly referred to war as the single most vexing problem threatening the nation and to international reconciliation as the goal of first priority on the nation's agenda. In the unending quest for reconciliation, higher education plays an important role. Colleges and universities are among the principal agencies through which any nation achieves understanding and rapport with the peoples of the world. They serve in this capacity in several ways.

First, academic people the world over are closely and continuously linked through research and scholarship. This linkage occurs through the exchange of publications and also through innumerable personal contacts among scientists and scholars as they correspond and as they meet in international gatherings and in private encounters.

Second, nations depend on their academic scholars for much of their understanding of the history, culture, languages, economics, and geography of other countries. Many universities support scholars who are specialists in particular foreign areas and some maintain interdisciplinary institutes or "area studies" programs for research on particular areas of the world.

Third, colleges and universities train most of the diplomats, military officers, journalists, and business leaders whose professional work requires knowledge of foreign peoples and government.

Fourth, colleges and universities carry on programs of technical assistance to other countries in fields such as agriculture, health, industrial technology, natural resource development, and education. And they supply training staff for technical assistance programs conducted by government, business, or other agencies.

Fifth, colleges and universities the world over are involved in international exchange of students and faculty.

American higher education has long served in these five ways and has regularly facilitated communication and understanding between America and the other nations of the world. These activities go on year in and year out. As a result, at any given time there are many thousands, perhaps millions, of Americans who have during their lives been in touch with foreign research and scholarship, have worked abroad under academic auspices in programs of technical assistance, have studied or taught abroad, or otherwise have gained knowledge and understanding of foreign countries. And there are comparable numbers of foreigners who have had similar contacts with the United States. Both sides in this interchange have on the whole achieved a deeper understanding and a keener appreciation of one or more foreign countries than would otherwise have been possible.

There is a sixth academic function that may be more important to international reconciliation than the others combined, namely, teaching rank-and-file American students about the nations and peoples of the world—helping them to gain perspective on the world about them, to achieve understanding and appreciation of other peoples, to form some conception of world problems and dilemmas, and to acquire a cosmopolitan outlook. It is this sixth type of international communication that pertains especially to the subject of educational possibilities for our grandchildren. A suitable education for people who will live in the dangerous twenty-first century should not neglect to prepare them for world citizenship. An appropriate education for them, as Stephen Bailey has reminded us, is one "that reaches out for friends in the vast threatening environment that surrounds us" (quoted by Harlan Cleveland, 1980, p. 22).

American higher education has, of course, long been concerned with international education. But its scope has been quite limited. It has concentrated largely on the antecedents of American culture. The study of subjects such as Western European history or Western European languages has been taught more as a foundation for the understanding of the American heritage than as the basis of a cosmopolitan or world outlook. Contact with the history, cultures, and languages of Eastern Europe, the Middle East, Africa, or the Far East has been sparse. Many institutions have indeed offered courses in international politics, international economics, studies of particular foreign areas, and the like. Also, many institutions have generated extracurricular programs relating to world affairs, for example, public lectures, chapel programs, international relations clubs, and pacifist activities. Yet, on the whole, the efforts to reach out beyond America have been feeble and student participation has been minimal. Indeed, in recent years the situation has deteriorated

as foreign language requirements and foreign language teaching
have diminished, and as vocational subjects have increasingly domi-
nated the curricula.

The prospective conditions of the twenty-first century call for
a citizenry and a leadership in America with understanding and
appreciation of foreign languages and cultures. But this does not
lessen the continuing need for a solid grounding in American civilization. To meet both these objectives within the limits of present
secondary and college programs, given the many demands on student time, is no simple matter. But it must be done. (For an
extended discussion of these matters, see the report of the President's
Commission on Foreign Languages and International Studies, 1979.
This commission was chaired by James A. Perkins.) As I see the
practical possibilities for undergraduate foreign studies, they would
be offered at three different tiers.

In the first tier, the common core of subjects taken by all
students would be studies in descriptive world geography with special attention to ethnography, culture, economy, and international
relations. (See the proposed curriculum presented in Chapter
Seven.) These studies would be reinforced by extracurricular programs relating to world affairs. The objective of the common core
would be general literacy about the world in which we live. Ideally,
every student would partake of such a core partly in high school and
partly in college. Each institution would design its program, however, around its own clientele, its own capabilities, and its unique
style.

In the second tier there would be a range of elective courses
relating to world cultures and world affairs. Most students would
elect some of these courses, which might be offered by various disciplines in the humanities, arts, social studies, foreign languages, and
even natural sciences. They would provide an opportunity for students to pursue their own special interests, for example, to delve
more deeply into a particular culture or to pursue comparative studies in a particular discipline.

In the third tier, some students—perhaps as many as one
fourth—would elect to study in some depth a particular area of the
world. These students would, of course, study an appropriate foreign language. Such language study would be an intensive effort

resulting in a reading and speaking knowledge of the chosen language, not merely in the kind of minimal competency that has been the result of most language study in the past. In addition, these students might organize their major fields around the chosen areas. For example, they might combine economics and Latin America, or literature and Japan, or art and Africa, or political science and East Europe, and so on. Many of these students would pursue part of their work in residence abroad.

For this three-tier pattern to function satisfactorily, it would be desirable, perhaps essential, that every college or university offer at least one program of study relating to a foreign area other than Western Europe and that these programs be distributed throughout the country in such a way that every part of the world would be adequately represented by at least a few study programs in American institutions. If such a distribution of area study programs were achieved, a substantial minority of American people could become versed in the language and culture of virtually every part of the world. In the present era of multinational corporations, international tourism, and increasing intergovernmental relationships, a background in area studies and languages is a valuable asset for careers.

But to achieve widespread international understanding would call for more than tinkering with the curriculum. It would require also that all education be conducted on the premise that the relevant community is not only the local neighborhood, or city, or state, or nation but also the world and that all subjects should be taught within the context of a world community. As Harlan Cleveland (1980, p. 19) wrote: "But competent American citizenship in an interdependent world cannot come from stuffing into the schools' curricula another course or two about foreign areas and faraway cultures. It will come from a generation of students relearning in each course they take, on every subject, at every level of education, that the world is round (and fully packed, too)—that everything Americans do or do not do affects the rest of the world, and everything others do bears watching for its effect on our own lives, our own purposes, and our own destiny."

As Cleveland implies, international education is not only a means toward international reconciliation, but also a tool of national defense. Our colleges and universities are a factor in the military power of the nation. Many of them conduct scientific research and scholarly inquiry that are applicable to national defense and to foreign affairs. Many also help to educate military personnel and specialists in foreign affairs. And in time of war, many are called upon to train members of the armed services. The academic community is, in a sense, part of the military establishment. Yet in the long run, the security of the nation lies in international reconciliation among peoples, which can only come about through understanding. And education is one of the principal means to that understanding.

Concluding Comments

In this book we have examined the state of higher education as it emerged from the several decades of immense growth that followed World War II. We have also examined the state of the nation as it entered the 1980s. From these two appraisals, we have deduced some of the more urgent long-term objectives of the nation and some of the more urgent responsibilities of higher education in fulfilling these objectives. The findings for the nation are that the objectives of highest priority lie in conservation and in the development of human resources. These objectives are far more urgent than the routine economic goals that command most of the attention of political leaders. And the findings for higher education are that the responsibilities of highest priority are (1) to strengthen and extend higher education so that America might become over several generations a nation of educated people; (2) to elevate the values of our people, individually and collectively, so that they might make better choices as citizens, as consumers, and as private individuals; (3) to redeem the lives of the millions of disadvantaged youth in America; and (4) to lay the groundwork for international reconciliation. This book is a plea for American higher education to increase its concern for the kind of people our children and grandchildren will become and the kind of world they will live in. The message of this book is that there is much urgent educational work to be done in the United States and that the years ahead are no time for retreat or retrenchment. The agenda calls for the higher educational community to expand present functions and to add new ones.

Unfortunately, the early 1980s is a time of uncertainty and pessimism among educators. They have already experienced or they fear demographic decline, reduced student aid funds, diminished appropriations, continuing inflation, and lukewarm popular and political support. Their goals range from sheer survival to maintenance of the status quo and seldom include ambitious new projects. Such a time of limitations would seem to be less than propitious for the advocacy of new responsibilities.

Yet, a higher educational system without a vision beyond next year's budget may be in a more precarious position than one that presents great plans that demonstrate the inadequacy of the present condition. Moreover, circumstances may change in ways that affect what higher education can achieve or become. For example, new technologies, new theories of economics and politics, new religious or philosophical movements, new levels of prosperity, depression, or war may alter the environment and the potential of higher education. Educators should not supinely accept the present situation as permanent, but should continually present new long-range possibilities to the public and their leaders.

Finally, as I have tried to show in a previous book (Bowen, 1980b), money is not everything in higher education. Our colleges and universities operate with very different budgets and with different outcomes. They vary greatly in efficiency. Many have resources that, with greater efficiency, would allow them to make progress toward the agenda identified in this book. Indeed, the justification for the relatively ample resources that some institutions possess is that they can provide leadership as the higher educational system sets out in new directions.

Appendix A ✤✤✤✤

Indicators of Economic and Social Progress in the United States, 1950-1980

The principal sources of the statistics presented in this appendix are as follows:

Economic Report of the President. Washington, D.C. U.S. Government Printing Office, annual.

Feldstein, M. (ed.). *The American Economy in Transition*. Chicago: University of Chicago Press, 1980.

National Center for Education Statistics, U.S. Department of Education. *Digest of Education Statistics*. Washington: U.S. Government Printing Office, annual.

Taeuber, C. (ed.). *America in the Seventies: Some Social Indicators*. Philadelphia: Annals of the American Academy of Political and Social Science, January 1978.

U.S. Bureau of the Census. *Historical Statistics of the United States: Colonial Times to 1970*. (2 vol). Washington, D.C.: U.S. Government Printing Office, 1975.

U.S. Bureau of the Census. *Social Indicators III*. Washington, D.C.: U.S. Government Printing Office, 1980.

U.S. Bureau of the Census. *Statistical Abstract of the United States*. Washington, D.C.: U.S. Government Printing Office, annual.

In many of the following tables, totals do not precisely add up to the sum of the components because decimals have been rounded off. The difference between the sums is inconsequential.

Table A1. The Population

	1950	1955	1960	1965	1970	1975	1979	Projected 2000	2050
Number (millions)[a]	152	166	181	194	205	214	221	260	316
Percentage distribution by age[b]									
Under 14	25%	—	30%	—	26%	23%	21%	20%	19%
14–17	6	—	6	—	8	8	7	6	5
18–24	11	—	9	—	12	13	13	9	9
25–64	50	—	46	—	44	46	47	52	49
65 and over	8	—	9	—	10	11	11	13	18
Total	100%	—	100%	—	100%	100%	100%	100%	100%
Dependency index: Those under 18 and over 64 as percentage of total population[c]									
Under 18	31%	—	36%	—	34%	31%	28%	26%	24%
Over 64	8	—	9	—	10	11	11	13	18
Total	39%	—	45%	—	44%	42%	39%	39%	42%
Urbanization: Percentage of the population resident in metropolitan areas[c]	56%	—	63%	—	69%	73%	73%[d]	—	—

[a] U.S. Bureau of the Census, *Statistical Abstract of the United States* (1980, pp. 6–7); projections are from Series II of the U.S. Census assuming replacement level fertility.

[b] *Statistical Abstract* (1980, pp. 30–31).

[c] *Statistical Abstract* (1980, p. 17).

[d] 1978.

Table A2. Production Trends

	1950	1955	1960	1965	1970	1975	1979
GNP (in billions of constant 1972 dollars)[a]	535	658	737	929	1,086	1,234	1,483
GNP per capita (in constant 1972 dollars)[b]	3,517	3,962	4,078	4,765	5,248	5,630	6,494
GNP per member of the labor force (in constant 1972 dollars)[c]	8,369	9,655	10,225	12,038	12,638	13,016	14,124
GNP per employed person (in constant 1972 dollars)[c]	8,825	10,084	10,794	12,592	13,271	14,183	14,980
Output per unit of capital and labor employed (index, 1967 = 100)[d]	63	73	80	95	104	110	114
Index of Industrial Production (1967 = 100)[e]	45	59	66	90	108	118	153
New construction (billions of 1972 dollars)[f]	78	92	93	110	107	97	115
Index of total farm output (1967 = 100)[g]	74	82	91	98	101	114	129
Index of farm output per unit of input (1967 = 100)[g]	71	78	90	100	102	115	119

[a] *Economic Report of the President* (1981, p. 234).

[b] U.S. Bureau of the Census, *Statistical Abstract of the United States* (1979, p. 438; 1980, p. 440).

[c] Computed from data in *Economic Report* (1981, pp. 234, 264).

[d] Grayson (1980, p. 39).

[e] *Economic Report* (1981, p. 278).

[f] *Statistical Abstract* (1980, p. 782); U.S. Bureau of the Census, *Historical Statistics of the United States*, Vol. 2 (1975, p. 618).

[g] *Economic Report* (1981, p. 338).

Table A3. Production: Composition of the Gross National Product

	1950	1955	1960	1965	1970	1975	1979
Percentage Breakdown by Industry[a]							
Agriculture, forestry, fisheries	7.3%	5.0%	4.2%	3.5%	2.9%	3.5%	3.3%
Construction	4.5	4.6	4.6	4.8	4.9	4.4	4.6
Manufacturing	29.3	30.3	28.4	28.4	25.5	22.9	23.6
Transportation, communications, utilities	9.0	8.9	9.1	8.8	8.7	8.8	9.0
Wholesale and retail trade	17.9	16.6	16.7	16.4	17.0	17.6	16.8
Finance, insurance and real estate	10.9	12.3	13.9	13.9	14.3	13.9	14.0
Services	8.4	8.5	9.7	10.3	11.6	12.2	12.8
Government and government enterprises[b]	8.3	9.6	10.6	11.2	13.1	13.1	11.8
All other[c]	4.4	4.2	2.8	2.8	2.0	3.7	4.1
Total	100.0%	100.0%	100.0%	100.0%	100.0%	100.0%	100.0%
Percentage Breakdown by Type of Product[d]							
Personal consumption expenditures							
Durable goods	8.1%	8.0%	7.1%	7.9%	8.3%	9.4%	9.9%
Nondurable goods	30.3	28.1	28.3	26.4	26.3	25.5	23.9
Services	24.9	24.1	26.1	26.0	27.7	29.6	29.0
Subtotal	63.3	60.3	61.5	60.3	62.3	64.5	61.8
Private domestic investment							
Nonresidential	9.4	9.4	9.0	10.3	10.0	9.5	11.0
Residential	6.2	5.4	4.8	4.7	3.8	3.2	4.0
Changes in business inventories	2.0	1.2	0.6	1.2	0.4	-0.8	0.7
Subtotal	17.6	16.0	14.4	16.2	14.4	11.9	15.7
Net exports	0.7	0.7	0.8	0.9	0.1	1.9	2.5
Government purchases of goods and services[b]							
Federal	8.8	13.3	12.3	10.9	10.3	8.0	6.9
State and local	9.5	9.8	11.1	11.8	13.0	13.8	12.1
Subtotal	18.3	23.1	23.4	22.7	23.3	21.8	19.0
Grand Total	100.0%	100.0%	100.0%	100.0%	100.0%	100.0%	100.0%
Gross government expenditures as percentage of GNP[b]	21%	25%	27%	27%	31%	34%	31%[c]

[a] U.S. Bureau of the Census, *Statistical Abstract of the United States* (1979, p. 439; 1980, p. 441). The industry classification is on an establishment, not company, basis.

Table A3 (Continued)

[b] "Government and Government Enterprises" refers to production carried on by capital and labor actually employed in government. This figure does not reflect the true cost of government because it excludes government purchases of goods from other industries. The true cost of government is shown by the figures on "Government purchases of goods and services." The figures on "Gross government expenditures" includes these costs and also transfer payments.

[c] Includes mining, rest of the world, and statistical residual.

[d] *Economic Report of the President* (1981, pp. 234–235).

[e] *Statistical Abstract* (1980, p. 261).

Table A4. International Investment Position of the United States
(in billions of dollars)

	1950	1955	1960	1965	1970	1975	1979
U.S. assets abroad	54.4	65.1	85.6	120.4	165.5	295.1	513.2
Foreign assets in the United States	17.6	27.8	40.9	58.8	106.8	220.5	418.2
U.S. net position:							
current dollars	36.7	37.2	44.7	61.6	58.6	74.6	95.0
constant 1972 dollars	68.5	61.1	65.1	82.8	64.1	59.4	48.4

Note: These figures are from the U.S. Bureau of the Census, *Statistical Abstract of the United States* (1979, p. 850; 1980, p. 863) and *Economic Report of the President* (1981, p. 349).

Table A5. The Labor Force

	1950	1955	1960	1965	1970	1975	1979
Noninstitutional population 16 years of age and over (millions)[a]	107	113	120	129	140	153	164
Civilian labor force (millions)[a]	62	65	70	74	83	93	103
Employment (millions)[a]	59	62	66	71	79	85	97
Unemployment (millions)[a]	3	3	4	3	4	8	6
Unemployment as percentage of civilian labor force[a]							
All ages	5%	4%	6%	5%	5%	9%	6%
Persons 16–19	12	11	15	15	15	20	16
Civilian labor force as percentage of civilian noninstitutional population 16 years of age and over[a]							
Men	86%	85%	83%	81%	80%	78%	78%
Women	34	36	38	39	43	46	51
Total	59%	59%	59%	59%	60%	61%	64%
Women in the labor force as percentage of female population 16 years of age and over[b]							
Single	51%	46%	44%	41%	53%	57%	63%
All married	25	29	32	36	41	45	50
Married, husband present	24	28	31	35	41	44	49
Widowed or divorced	36	36	37	36	36	38	40
Total, all women	34%	36%	38%	39%	43%	46%	51%

[a] *Economic Report of the President* (1981, pp. 264, 267).
[b] U.S. Bureau of the Census, *Statistical Abstract of the United States* (1981, p. 402).

Table A6. The Labor Force: Employment by Type of Work

	1950	1960	1965	197	1975	1979
White-collar workers						
Professional and						
technical	8%	11%	13%	14%	15%	16%
Managers and ad-						
ministrators	11	11	10	11	11	11
Salesworkers	7	6	6	6	6	6
Clerical workers	13	15	16	17	18	18
Subtotal	38	43	45	48	49	51
Blue-collar workers						
Craft and kindred						
workers	13	13	13	13	13	13
Operatives	20	18	19	18	15	15
Nonfarm laborers	6	5	5	5	5	5
Subtotal	39	37	37	35	33	33
Service workers	11	12	13	12	14	13
Farm workers	12	8	6	4	3	3
Grand total	100%	100%	100%	100%	100%	100%

U.S. Bureau of the Census, *Statistical Abstract of the United States* (1980, p. 418; 1977, p. 406).

Table A7. The Standard of Living: Personal Income and Expenditure

	1950	1955	1960	1965	1970	1975	1979
Disposable personal income per capita (constant 1972 dollars)[a]	2,393	2,583	2,709	3,171	3,668	4,101	4,584
Median income of families (constant 1979 dollars)[b]	9,965[c]	11,976	13,774	16,005	18,444	18,502	19,684
Personal consumption expenditures: Percentage distribution by type of product[d]							
Food, beverage, tobacco	30.3%	28.5%	27.1%	24.9%	23.8%	22.9%	21.3%
Clothing, accessories, jewelry	12.3	11.0	9.9	9.4	9.0	8.4	7.8
Personal care	1.3	1.4	1.6	1.8	1.8	1.5	1.3
Housing	11.3	13.5	14.8	15.2	15.2	15.3	16.0
Household operation	15.2	14.6	14.2	14.2	14.2	14.5	14.5
Medical care expenses	4.7	5.2	6.2	7.0	8.1	9.1	9.7
Personal business	3.4	3.7	4.4	4.6	5.1	5.3	5.4
Transportation	13.2	13.6	13.1	13.5	12.6	12.8	14.1
Recreation	5.8	5.6	5.5	6.0	6.6	6.8	6.8
Other	2.4	2.9	3.3	3.4	3.7	3.4	3.2
Total	100.0%	100.0%	100.0%	100.0%	100.0%	100.0%	100.0%
Durable goods	12.6%	13.0%	11.4%	13.0%	13.3%	14.5%	15.8%
Nondurable goods	48.0	47.0	46.1	43.8	42.2	39.5	38.1
Services	39.4	40.0	42.6	43.2	44.5	46.1	46.2
Total	100.0%	100.0%	100.0%	100.0%	100.0%	100.0%	100.0%

[a] *Economic Report of the President* (1981, p. 259).
[b] *Economic Report* (1981, p. 262).
[c] Estimated by the author.
[d] U.S. Bureau of the Census, *Statistical Abstract of the United States* (1980, p. 442); *Economic Report* (1981, p. 234).

Table A8. The Standard of Living: Percentage Distribution of GNP, by Functional Use

	1952	1955	1966	1969	1973	1977
Basic necessities	48.0%	44.7%	38.0%	37.0%	35.3%	35.5%
Education and manpower	3.6	4.3	6.4	7.1	7.6	7.8
Health	4.3	4.6	5.9	6.6	7.4	8.5
Transportation	10.0	11.5	11.3	11.3	11.4	11.7
General government	2.3	2.2	2.8	3.1	3.5	3.9
Defense	12.8	9.3	7.9	8.1	5.6	4.9
New housing	5.3	6.0	4.0	4.2	5.2	5.0
Business investment	9.9	11.1	12.7	11.6	11.8	10.9
Other	3.9	6.5	11.0	11.1	12.1	11.8
Total	100.0%	100.0%	100.0%	100.0%	100.0%	100.0%

Source: Ripley (1980, p. 5).

Table A9. The Standard of Living: Housing and Household Equipment

	1950	1960	1965	1970	1975	1979
Housing units, median number of rooms[a]	—	4.9	—	5.0	—	5.1[d]
Percentage of housing units owner occupied[b]	55%	62%	—	63%	65%	65%[d]
Percentage of housing units with:[a, c]						
Telephone	—	79	—	87	—	91[d]
Air conditioning	—	12	—	37	—	54[d]
Air conditioning central system	—	2	—	11	—	24[d]
One or more automobiles	—	78	—	83	—	84[d]
Public sewer	—	—	—	70	—	73[d]
Public or private water company	—	—	—	82	—	84[d]
Dishwasher	—	7	14	27	38	43
Clothes washer	—	55	57	62	70	77
Clothes dryer	—	20	26	45	58	62
Freezer	—	23	27	31	44	45
Refrigerator	—	98	100	100	100	100
Color TV	—	—	10	43	74	90
Microwave oven	—	—	—	—	3	8

[a]U.S. Bureau of the Census, *Statistical Abstract of the United States* (1980, p. 791.
[b]*Statistical Abstract* (1980, p. 793).
[c]*Statistical Abstract* (1980, p. 796).
[d]1978.

Table A10. The Standard of Living: Participation in Leisure and Recreation

	1960	1965	1970	1975	1979
Visits to national parks (millions)[a]	79	121	172	239	282
Visits to state parks (millions)[b]	259	391	483	566	596
Visits to national forests (millions)[c]	—	—	—	—	220
Fishing and hunting licenses sold (millions)[d]	42	44	53	61	59
U.S. passports for foreign travel for pleasure, personal reasons (millions)[e]	2		35	6	8
Amateur softball players (millions)[f]	—	—	16	26	30
Golfers playing 15 rounds or more (millions)[f]	4	8	10	12	13
Tennis players (millions)[f]	5	—	11	34	32
Bicycles purchased (millions)[f]	4	6	7	14	11
Recreational boats owned (millions)[f]	7	8	9	10	12
Attendance at selected spectator sports (millions)[g]					
Major league baseball	20	22	29	30	44
College basketball	—	—	—	—	30
Professional basketball	2	3	7	11	11
College football	20	25	29	32	35
Professional football	4	7	10	11	14
Professional soccer	—	—	—	2	6
Horseracing	47	63	70	79	74
Greyhound racing	8	11	13	17	21
Personal consumption expenditures for recreation (billions of constant 1967 dollars)[h]	20	27	35	41	47
Average hours per week devoted to leisure time[i]	—	35	—	39	—
Median hours per day spent viewing television[i]	2.3	2.6	2.8	2.9	3.1

[a] U.S. Bureau of the Census, *Statistical Abstract of the United States* (1980, p. 242).

[b] *Statistical Abstract* (1980, p. 244).

[c] *Statistical Abstract* (1980, p. 243).

[d] *Statistical Abstract* (1980, p. 247).

[e] *Statistical Abstract* (1980, p. 252).

[f] *Statistical Abstract* (1980, p. 246).

[g] *Statistical Abstract* (1980, p. 248).

[h] *Statistical Abstract* (1980, p. 245).

[i] U.S. Bureau of the Census, *Social Indicators III* (1980, pp. 559–561); dates are approximate.

Table A11. The Physical Environment: Use and Conservation of Resources

	1950	1955	1960	1965	1970	1975	1979
Energy							
Total consumption per capita (millions of Btu)[a]	223	240	245	274	328	332	354
U.S. consumption of energy as percentage of world consumption[b]	—	—	35%	34%	33%	30%	29%[i]
U.S. production of energy as percentage of U.S. consumption[c]	101%	98%	95%	94%	94%	85%	81%
Electricity generated with nuclear power (billions of kilowatt hours)[d]	—	—	—	4	22	173	255
Average speed of motor vehicles, mph[e]	—	—	55	61	64	58	59
Water used (gallons per capita)[f]							
Total, daily average	1,340	—	1,787	1,390	1,816	1,582	—
Ground water only	230	—	321	252	337	384	—
Quantity of materials used							
Domestic intercity freight traffic (ton miles per capita)[g]	7,183	7,824	7,360	8,497	9,449	9,672	11,149[i]
Solid waste disposal, net, per person per day (in pounds)[h]	—	—	2.5	2.8	3.3	3.3	3.5[i]

[a] U.S. Bureau of the Census, *Statistical Abstract of the United States* (1980, p. 604); Btu = British thermal units.

[b] *Statistical Abstract* (1979, p. 603; 1980, p. 606).

[c] *Statistical Abstract* (1980, p. 603).

[d] *Statistical Abstract* (1980, p. 620).

[e] *Statistical Abstract* (1980, p. 646).

[f] *Statistical Abstract* (1980, p. 213).

[g] *Statistical Abstract* (1980, p. 639).

[h] *Statistical Abstract* (1980, p. 218).

[i] 1978.

Table A12. The Physical Environment: Pollution

	1965	1970	1975	1979
Air pollution				
Estimates of national emissions from all sources (millions of short tons)[a]				
Particulates	—	25.6	16.1	13.8[f]
Sulfur oxides	—	32.8	28.9	29.8[f]
Nitrogen oxides	—	21.9	23.0	25.7[f]
Hydrocarbons	—	31.2	27.9	30.6[f]
Carbon monoxide	—	113.1	107.1	112.5[f]
Motor vehicle pollutant emissions (grams per vehicle mile)[b]				
Carbon monoxide	—	86.9	77.0	65.2
Hydrocarbons	—	12.1	9.4	7.3
Nitrogen oxide	—	4.7	4.6	3.8
Percentage of cars with one or more emission controls[b]	54%	85%	96%	98%
Water pollution				
Percentage of population served by sewage treatment system[c]	22%	42%	—	69%
Polluting discharges reported in U.S. waters[c]				
Number of incidents (thousands)	—	10	12	14[f]
Gallons (millions)	—	19	15	17[f]
Production of synthetic organic pesticides (millions of pounds)[d]	877	1,034	1,603	1,416[f]
Discharged commercial reactor fuel[e]				
Annual discharge (tons)	—	67	547	1,390
Inventory, year end (tons)	—	161	1,584	5,746

[a] U.S. Bureau of the Census, *Statistical Abstract of the United States* (1980, p. 217)

[b] *Statistical Abstract* (1979, p. 649).

[c] *Statistical Abstract* (1980, p. 218).

[d] *Statistical Abstract* (1980, p. 219).

[e] *Statistical Abstract* (1980, p. 620).

[f] 1978.

Table A13. The Physical Environment: National Expenditures for the Abatement and Control of Pollution (billions of 1972 dollars)

	1957	1960	1965	1972	1975	1978
Pollution abatement						
Individuals	—	—	—	1.6	2.6	3.0
Businesses	—	—	—	11.1	12.7	14.5
Government	—	—	—	4.8	6.0	6.6
Subtotal	—	—	—	17.5	21.3	24.1
Regulation and monitoring	—	—	—	0.4	0.5	0.6
Research and development	—	—	—	0.8	0.8	1.0
Total	—	—	—	18.7	22.6	25.7
Outlays for municipal waste-water treatment (in millions of 1967 dollars)[a]	45	74	151	—	1,202	1,953

Note: The source for this table is U.S. Bureau of the Census, *Statistical Abstract of the United States* (1979, p. 210; 1980, p. 214).
[a] Advisory Commission on Intergovernmental Relations (1981, p. 26).

Table A14. Conditions of Work

	1950	1955	1960	1965	1970	1975	1978
Satisfied workers as percentage of all workers[a]							
Male	—	—	84[b,g]	92[c,h]	86[d,i]	90	85
Female	—	—	81[b,g]	—	86[d,i]	87	83
White	—	—	84[b,g]	92[c,h]	87[di]	89	84
Black	—	—	76[b,g]	88[c,h]	78[d,i]	85	81
Labor turnover in manufacturing per month per 100 employees[b]							
Separations	—	—	4.3	4.1	4.8	4.2	4.0[j]
Quits	—	—	1.3	1.9	2.1	1.4	2.0[j]
Deaths and injuries per 100,000 workers from industrial accidents[c]							
Deaths	27	24	21	20	17	15	14
Disabling injuries	3,311	3,135	2,964	2,954	2,799	2,594	2,331
Labor union membership as percentage of nonagricultural wage and salary workers[d]	29%	32%	30%	28%	27%	26%	24%
Work stoppages (strikes)[e]							
Number	4,843	4,320	3,333	3,963	5,176	5,031	4,230
Percentage of employed workers involved	5.1%	5.2%	2.4%	2.5%	4.7%	2.2%	1.9%
Average weekly hours in nonagricultural establishments[f]	39.8	39.6	38.6	38.8	37.1	36.1	35.7[j]

[a] U.S. Bureau of the Census, *Statistical Abstract of the United States* (1978, p. 402; 1980, p. 405).
[b] *Statistical Abstract* (1980, p. 405).
[c] *Statistical Abstract* (1980, p. 433).
[d] *Statistical Abstract* (1980, p. 429).
[e] *Statistical Abstract* (1980, p. 431).
[f] *Statistical Abstract* (1980, p. 411).
[g] 1962.
[h] 1964.
[i] 1972.
[j] 1979.

Table A15. Distribution of Personal Income Among Families

	1950	1955	1960	1965	1970	1975	1977	1978
Percentage of income received, by income level (in constant 1977 dollars)[a]								
Under $5,000	25%	20%	17%	13%	8%	10%	9%	—
5,000– 6,999	14	10	9	8	7	7	7	—
7,000– 9,999	24	20	15	13	11	12	11	—
10,000–11,999	20	15	15	10	8	8	7	—
12,000–14,999	11	13	13	15	13	12	11	—
15,000–19,999	5	13	17	21	23	18	18	—
20,000–24,999	1	5	6	9	11	14	14	—
25,000 and over	1	4	7	12	18	19	22	—
Total	100%	100%	100%	100%	100%	100%	100%	—
Percentage of income received by designated fraction of families[b]								
Lowest fifth	4.5%	4.8%	4.8%	5.2%	5.4%	5.4%	5.2%	5.2%
Highest fifth	42.7	41.3	41.3	40.9	40.9	41.1	41.5	41.5
Highest 5 percent	17.3	16.4	15.9	15.5	15.6	15.5	15.7	15.6
Percentage of families with incomes below the poverty level[c]	—	—	18.1%	13.9%	10.1%	9.7%	—	9.1%[e]
Percentage of population in income poverty[d]								
Before cash transfers	—	—	—	21%	—	21%[f]	—	—
After cash transfers	32%[g]	—	—	16	—	11[f]	—	—
After cash and in-kind transfers	—	—	—	12	—	7[f]	—	—

[a] U.S. Bureau of the Census, *Statistical Abstract of the United States* (1979, p. 448; 1980, p. 450).
[b] *Statistical Abstract* (1980, p. 454).
[c] *Economic Report of the President* (1981, p. 262).
[d] Danziger and Lampman (1978, p. 28). *In-kind transfers* refer to food stamps, housing subsidies, education subsidies, and so on.
[e] 1979.
[f] 1976.
[g] 1947.

Table A16. Distribution of National Income by Sources

	1950	1955	1960	1965	1970	1975	1979
Compensation of employees	66%	68%	72%	70%	76%	77%	76%
Wages and salaries	62	65	66	64	69	66	64
Supplements	3	4	6	6	8	10	12
Proprietor's income	16	13	11	10	8	7	7
Farm	6	3	3	2	2	2	2
Nonfarm	11	10	9	8	6	5	5
Rental income	3	3	3	3	2	2	1
Corporate profits	14	14	11	14	9	8	9
Net interest	1	2	2	3	5	7	7
Total	100%	100%	100%	100%	100%	100%	100%

Note: The source of the data in this table is *Economic Report of the President* (1981, pp. 254-255).

Table A17. Inflation

	1950	1955	1960	1965	1970	1975	1979
Implicit price deflator for GNP (1967 = 100)[a]	68	77	87	94	116	161	209
Consumer Price Index (1967 = 100)[b]	72	80	89	95	116	161	217
Producer Price Index (1967 = 100)[c]	82	88	95	97	110	175	236

[a] *Economic Report of the President* (1981, p. 236).
[b] *Economic Report* (1981, p. 296).
[c] U.S. Bureau of the Census, *Statistical Abstract of the United States* (1980, p. 479).

Table A18. Social Welfare: Expenditures

	1950	1960	1965	1970	1975	1978
Public and private expenditures for social welfare as percentage of GNP[a]						
Income maintenance	4.0%	6.0%	6.5%	7.5%	10.5%	10.2%
Health	4.5	5.2	5.9	7.2	8.4	9.2
Education	4.1	4.4	5.2	6.4	6.6	6.1
Welfare and other services	0.8	0.5	0.7	1.0	1.7	2.0
Total	13.4%	15.8%	17.9%	21.8%	26.7%	26.9%
Public and private expenditures for social welfare in constant 1967 dollars per capita[a,b]						
Income maintenance	97	186	232	304	443	489
Health	109	162	212	290	355	438
Education	101	136	185	259	280	291
Welfare and other services	18	17	24	41	72	94
Total	322	491	642	878	1,150	1,313
Public expenditures for social welfare as percentage of the total outlay of government[a]						
Federal	26%	28%	33%	40%	54%	56%
State and local	59	60	60	64	65	66
Combined	37%	38%	42%	48%	58%	60%

[a] U.S. Bureau of the Census, *Statistical Abstract of the United States* (1980, pp. 330–331).

[b] Deflated using Consumer Price Index, 1967 = 100.

Table A19. Social Welfare: Philanthropy

	1950	1955	1960	1965	1970	1975	1979
Private philanthropy							
Funds raised[a]							
Current dollars							
(billions)	—	—	9.4	13.3	20.7	29.7	43.3
Constant 1967 dollars							
(billions)	—	—	10.6	14.1	17.8	18.4	19.9
Funds raised as percentage of GNP	—	—	1.9%	1.9%	2.1%	1.9%	1.8%
Volunteer workers							
(millions)	—	—	—	24.3	—	36.8[e]	—
Value of volunteer services (billions of 1974 dollars)[b]	—	—	—	22.9	46.3	67.8[e]	—
Voluntary support for colleges and universities[c]							
Current dollars							
(billions)	0.2	—	—	1.4	1.9	2.2	3.8[f]
Constant 1967 dollars							
(billions)	0.3	—	—	1.5	1.6	1.4	1.6[f]
U.S. government foreign economic aid[d]							
Billions of current dollars	4.4[g]	2.7[h]	—	4.1	3.7	4.9	6.9
Billions of constant 1967 dollars	6.2[g]	3.2[h]	—	4.3	3.2	3.0	3.2
As percentage of GNP	1.5%	0.7%	—	0.6%	0.4%	0.3%	0.3%

[a] U.S. Bureau of the Census, *Statistical Abstract of the United States* (1980, p. 363).

[b] U.S. Bureau of the Census, *Social Indicators III* (1980, p. 519).

[c] *Chronicle of Higher Education* (May 18, 1981, p. 8).

[d] *Statistical Abstract* (1980, p. 870).

[e] 1974.

[f] 1980.

[g] Mean 1946–1952.

[h] Mean 1953–1961.

Table A20. The Family

	1950	1955	1960	1965	1970	1975	1979
Families by type, percentages[a]							
Husband-wife	88%	87%	87%	87%	87%	84%	83%
Female head, no husband present	9	10	10	11	11	13	15
Male head, no wife present	3	3	3	3	2	3	3
Total	100%	100%	100%	100%	100%	100%	100%
Average size of families[a]	3.54	3.59	3.67	3.70	3.58	3.42	3.31
Marriages per 1,000 population[b]	11	9	9	9	11	10	11
Married persons as percentage of population 18 years and over[c]	67%	—	67%	73%	72%	70%	66%
First marriages of brides per thousand single women 18–24 years old[b]	—	—	472	404	372	259	219[h]
Divorces per 1,000 population[b]	3	2	2	3	4	5	5
Divorces per 1,000 married women 15 years old and over[b]	10	9	9	11	15	20	22[h]
Estimated number of children involved in divorces[b]	—	347	463	630	870	1,123	1,147[h]
Births per 1,000 population[d]	24	25	24	19	18	15	16
Premarital births as percent of all births[e]	4%	5%	5%	8%	11%	14%	16%
Legal abortions per 1,000 white women 15–44 years old[f]	—	—	—	—	12[i]	17	23[h]
Percentage of married women (husband present) in the labor force[g]	24%	28%	31%	35%	41%	44%	49%

[a] U.S. Bureau of the Census, *Statistical Abstract of the United States* (1980, p. 45).

[b] *Statistical Abstract* (1980, p. 83); includes first and subsequent marriages.

[c] *Statistical Abstract* (1980, p. 41).   [d] *Statistical Abstract* (1980, p. 61).

[e] *Statistical Abstract* (1980, p. 66).   [f] *Statistical Abstract* (1980, p. 69).

[g] *Statistical Abstract* (1980, p. 403).   [h] 1978.   [i] 1972.

Table A21. Longevity and Health: Selected Indexes

	1950	1955	1960	1965	1970	1975	1978
Expectation of life at birth (average in years)[a]	68.2	69.6	69.7	70.2	70.9	72.5	73.8[h]
Deaths (per 1,000 population)[b]	9.6	9.3	9.5	9.4	9.5	8.9	8.8
Infant deaths (per 1,000 live births)[c]	29.2	26.4	26.0	24.7	20.0	16.1	13.8
Suicides (per 100,000 population)[d]	11.4	10.2	10.6	11.1	11.6	12.7	12.5
Average height and weight of men 18–24 years of age[e]							
height (inches)	—	—	68.7	—	—	69.7	—
weight (pounds)	—	—	158	—	—	165	—
Persons with activity limitations due to chronic conditions (percentage of the civilian noninstitutional population)[f]	—	—	—	—	11.7	—	14.2
Days of disability per person[g]							
Restricted activity days	—	—	—	16.4	14.6	17.9	18.8
Bed disability days	—	—	—	6.2	6.1	6.6	7.1
Work-loss days	—	—	—	5.7	5.4	5.2	5.2
School-loss days	—	—	—	5.2	4.9	5.1	5.4

[a] U.S. Bureau of the Census, *Statistical Abstract of the United States* (1980, p. 72).
[b] *Statistical Abstract* (1980, p. 74).
[c] *Statistical Abstract* (1980, p. 77).
[d] *Statistical Abstract* (1980, p. 78).
[e] *Statistical Abstract* (1980, p. 125); data refer to 1960–1962 and 1971–1974.
[f] *Statistical Abstract* (1980, p. 127).
[g] *Statistical Abstract* (1980, p. 123).
[h] 1979.

Table A22. Longevity and Health: Reported Cases of Specified Diseases
(in thousands)

	1950	1955	1960	1965	1970	1975	1978
Amebiasis (dysentery)	4.6	3.3	3.4	2.8	2.9	2.8	3.9
Brucellosis	3.5	1.4	0.8	0.3	0.2	0.3	0.2
Diphtheria	5.8	2.0	0.9	0.2	0.4	0.3	0.1
Encephalitis	1.1	2.2	2.3	2.7	1.9	4.3	1.2
Gonorrhea	287.0	236.0	259.0	325.0	600.0	1,000.0	1,000.0
Hepatitis	2.8	32.0	41.7	33.9	65.1	56.2	53.3
Malaria	2.2	0.5	0.1	0.1	3.1	0.4	0.7
Measles	319.1	555.2	441.7	261.9	47.4	24.4	26.9
Meningococcal infections	3.8	3.5	2.3	3.0	2.5	1.5	2.5
Pertussis (whooping cough)	120.7	62.8	14.8	6.8	4.2	1.7	2.1
Poliomyelitis	33.3	29.0	3.2	0.1	—	—	—
Salmonellosis	1.2	5.4	6.9	17.2	22.1	22.6	29.4
Streptococcal sore throat and scarlet fever	64.5	147.5	315.2	295.2	433.4	330.8	397.0
Syphilis	218.0	122.0	122.0	113.0	91.0	80.0	65.0
Tetanus	0.5	0.5	0.4	0.3	0.1	0.1	0.1
Trichinosis	0.3	0.3	0.2	0.2	0.1	0.3	0.1
Tuberculosis	130.3[a]	76.2	55.5	49.0	37.1	34.0	28.5
Tularemia	0.9	0.6	0.4	0.3	0.2	0.1	0.2
Typhoid fever	2.5	1.7	0.8	0.5	0.3	0.4	0.5
Typhus fever (flea borne)	0.7	0.1	0.1	—	—	—	—
Typhus fever (tick borne)	0.5	0.3	0.2	0.3	0.4	0.8	1.1

[a] Estimate based on data in U.S. Bureau of the Census, *Historical Statistics of the United States*, Vol. 1 (1975, p. 77).

Source: These figures have been excerpted from U.S. Bureau of the Census, *Statistical Abstract of the United States* (1980, p. 126).

Table A23. Crime: Selected Indicators

	1950	1955	1960	1965	1970	1975	1979
Crimes known to the police: rate per 100,000 population[a]							
Violent crimes	—	—	—	253[h]	364	482	535
Property crimes	—	—	—	2,737[h]	3,621	4,800	4,986
Total	—	—	—	2,990[h]	3,985	5,282	5,521
Homicide victims: rate per 100,000 population[b]	5.2	4.5	4.7	5.5	8.3	10.0	9.4[h]
Criminal cases commenced (thousands)[c]							
U.S. court of appeals	0.3	—	0.6	1.2	2.7	4.2	4.1
U.S. district courts	—	—	28.1	31.6	38.1	41.1	31.5
Juvenile court cases per 1,000 population under 18[d]							
Delinquency cases	—	—	20.1	23.6	32.3	39.9	46.2[h]
Dependency and neglect cases	—	—	2.0	2.3	1.9	2.2	2.5[h]
Persons arrested: percentage female[e]	—	—	—	—	14.4	15.7	15.7
Federal and state prisons: prisoners per 100,000 population[f]	110	113	119	110	97	113	135[h]
Federal prosecutions of public corruption[g]							
Indictments	—	—	—	—	63	255	666
Convictions	—	—	—	—	44	179	536

[a] U.S. Bureau of the Census, *Statistical Abstract of the United States* (1980, p. 182).
[b] *Statistical Abstract* (1980, p. 186).
[c] *Statistical Abstract* (1980, p. 196).
[d] *Statistical Abstract* (1980, p. 199); excludes traffic violations.
[e] *Statistical Abstract* (1980, p. 190).
[f] *Statistical Abstract* (1980, p. 200).
[g] *Statistical Abstract* (1980, p. 195).
[h] 1968.

Table A24. Crime: By Age of Offender

	1950	1955	1960	1965	1970	1974	1978
Urban police arrests of suspected offenders by age: rate per 100,000 urban population[a]							
Crimes of violence:							
11–14 years old	—	—	70	99	164	195	—
15–17	—	—	273	323	524	675	—
18–24	—	—	358	380	550	703	—
25 and over	—	—	111	116	140	169	—
Total, all ages	—	—	144	163	232	292	—
Crimes of theft:							
11–14 years old	—	—	1,212	1,745	1,080	1,470	—
15–17	—	—	2,596	3,088	3,960	4,735	—
18–24	—	—	1,181	1,259	1,827	2,260	—
25 and over	—	—	207	227	295	345	—
Total, all ages	—	—	581	718	968	1,164	—
Persons arrested: percentage distribution by age[b]							
Under 18	4.4%	10.5%	14.3%	21.4%	25.3%	26.0%[c]	23.3%
18–24	26.2	16.1	17.8	20.9	27.2	31.0[c]	33.6
25–34	30.1	24.7	21.4	17.7	17.2	19.3[c]	21.8
35 and over	39.3	48.7	46.5	40.0	30.4	23.7[c]	21.9
Total	100.0%	100.0%	100.0%	100.0%	100.0%	100.0%[c]	100.0%

[a] Seidman (1978, pp. 264–266).
[b] U.S. Bureau of the Census, *Statistical Abstract of the United States* (1979, p. 185); *Historical Statistics of the United States*, Vol. 1 (1975, p. 415).
[c] 1975.

Table A25. Communications

	1950	1955	1960	1965	1970	1975	1979
Postal service, pieces of first class mail handled (billions)[a]	25	29	33	38	49	51	58
Telephones per 1,000 population[b]	256	301	365	422	512	609	677[l]
Average daily telephone conversation (millions)[c]	—	—	285	267	486	627	746
Number of overseas telephone calls (millions)[b]	1	1	3	8	23	62	134[l]
Number of radio stations[d]	2,229	2,742	3,688	4,279	4,898	5,535	5,648[l]
Number of TV stations[d]	107	437	530	588	686	693	714[l]
Number of cable TV systems[e]	—	400	640	1,325	2,490	3,506	4,150
Households with TV sets, as percentage of all households[e]	9%	65%	87%	93%	95%	97%	98%
Households with TV sets, average viewing per day, hours[e]	4.6	4.9	5.1	5.5	5.9	6.1	6.3
Number of newspapers, (thousands)[f]	12.1	11.4	11.3	11.4	11.4	11.4	9.8
Number of periodicals (thousands)[f]	7.0	7.6	8.4	9.0	9.6	9.7	9.7
Daily and Sunday newspapers, circulation per 1,000 people[g]	476	472	466	436	416	370	362[l]
Newsprint consumption per capita (pounds)[g]	—	—	77	83	90	87	100[l]
Copyright registrations (thousands)[h]	—	—	244	294	317	401	453[m]
New books and new editions published (thousands)[i]	—	—	15	29	36	39	45
Imports and translations of books (thousands)[j]	—	—	—	—	—	5.7	7.1
Advertising expenditures, 1972, dollars per capita[k]	70	90	96	106	104	105	138

[a] U.S. Bureau of the Census, *Statistical Abstract of the United States* (1980, p. 580).
[b] *Statistical Abstract* (1980, p. 583).
[c] *Statistical Abstract* (1980, p. 584).
[d] *Statistical Abstract* (1980, p. 586).
[e] *Statistical Abstract* (1980, p. 589).
[f] *Statistical Abstract* (1980, p. 591).
[g] *Statistical Abstract* (1980, p. 592).
[h] *Statistical Abstract* (1980, p. 594).
[i] *Statistical Abstract* (1980, p. 595).
[j] *Statistical Abstract* (1980, p. 596).
[k] *Statistical Abstract* (1980, p. 597).
[l] 1978.
[m] 1977.

Table A26. Voting

	1952	1956	1960	1964	1968	1972	1976	1980
Percentage of voting age population voting for:								
President	62%	59%	63%	62%	61%	56%	54%	53%
U.S. Representatives	58	56	59	58	55	51	50	45

Source: These figures are from the U.S. Bureau of the Census, Statistical Abstract of the United States (1980, p. 515)

Table A27. Education: Enrollment in Schools or Colleges

	1950	1955	1960	1965	1970	1975	1979
Enrollment (in millions)[a]							
Elementary-secondary education	28.0	35.0	42.7	49.0	53.0	51.3	47.9
Higher education	2.2	2.4	3.6	5.7	7.4	9.7	10.0
Total	30.2	37.4	46.3	54.7	60.4	61.0	57.9
Percentage of population enrolled, by ages[b]							
3–4 years	—	—	—	—	20.5%	31.5%	35.1%
5	51.8%	58.1%	63.7%	70.1%	77.7	87.2	91.6[c]
6	97.0	98.2	98.0	98.7	98.4	99.0	99.0[c]
7–13	98.8	99.2	99.6	99.4	99.3	99.3	99.2
14–15	94.7	95.9	97.8	98.9	98.1	98.2	98.1
16–17	71.3	77.4	82.6	87.4	90.0	89.0	89.2
18–19	29.4	31.5	38.4	46.3	47.7	46.9	45.0
20–24	9.0	11.1	13.1	19.0	21.5	22.4	21.7
25–29	3.0	4.2	4.9	6.1	7.5	10.1	9.4[c]
30–34	0.9	1.6	2.4	3.2	4.2	6.6	6.4[c]
Ages 5–34 combined	44.2	50.8	56.4	59.7	58.9	55.0	—

[a]U.S. Bureau of the Census, *Statistical Abstract of the United States* (1971, p. 104; 1980, p. 143).
[b]National Center for Education Statistics, *Digest of Education Statistics* (1976, p. 8); *Statistical Abstract* (1980, p. 145).
[c]1978.

Table A28. Education: Expenditures of Educational Institutions
(in constant 1967 dollars)

	1950	1960	1965	1970	1975	1979
Expenditures (billions)						
Elementary-secondary education	$ 9.3	$20.3	$31.8	$39.3	$44.8	$44.6
Higher education	2.9	7.6	16.0	21.2	24.1	25.1
Total	12.2	27.9	47.8	60.5	68.9	69.7
Total as percent of GNP	3.3%	5.0%	6.3%	7.3%	7.6%	6.7%
Expenditures per student enrolled						
Elementary-secondary education	$ 332	$ 476	$ 648	$ 741	$ 874	$ 932
Higher education	1,325	2,097	2,822	2,869	2,487	2,507

Source: These figures are from the U.S. Bureau of the Census, *Statistical Abstract of the United States* (1979, pp. 136–137; 1980, pp. 140–141).

Table A29. Educational Level of the Adult Population
(25 years of age and over)

	1950	1960	1970	1975	1979
Percentage distribution of the adult population, by years of school completed					
0-4 years	11.1%	8.3%	5.3%	4.2%	3.5%
5-7	16.4	13.8	9.1	7.4	6.2
8	20.8	17.5	13.4	10.3	8.6
9-11	17.4	19.2	17.1	15.6	14.0
12	20.8	24.6	34.0	36.2	36.6
13-15	7.4	8.8	10.2	12.4	14.7
16 or more	6.2	7.7	11.0	13.9	16.4
Total	100.0%	100.0%	100.0%	100.0%	100.0%
Median school years completed	9.3	10.6	12.2	12.3	12.5

Source: These figures are from U.S. Bureau of the Census, *Statistical Abstract of the United States* (1964, p. 113; 1980, p. 149).

Table A30. The Arts

	1960	1965	1970	1975	1979
Federal aid to the arts and humanities (millions)[a]	—	—	29	173	367
Attendance (millions)[b]					
Opera companies	—	—	4.6[e]	8.0	9.9
Major symphony orchestras	—	6.8	9.0	12.0	13.7
Legitimate theatres, Broadway and road, playing weeks[b]	1,884	1,893	2,071	1,900	2,664
Museum visits (millions)[b]	—	—	308[e]	—	—
Registration of copy-rights (thousands)[c]					
dramatic or dramatic-musical com-positions	2.4	3.3	3.4	4.9	5.5[f]
musical compositions	65.6	80.9	88.9	114.8	131.2[f]
works of art, models, designs	5.3	5.7	6.8	11.0	13.7[f]
reproduction of works of art	2.5	3.2	3.0	5.0	4.4[f]
motion picture photoplays	2.8	2.5	1.2	1.0	2.6[f]
motion pictures, not photoplays	.7	1.2	1.3	2.0	2.6[f]
sound recordings	—	—	—	8.9	10.6[f]
Imports of works of art and antiques (millions of dollars)[d]	73	141	162	677	1,487

[a] U.S. Bureau of the Census, *Statistical Abstract of the United States* (1980, p. 249).

[b] *Statistical Abstract* (1980, p. 250).

[c] *Statistical Abstract* (1980, p. 594).

[d] *Statistical Abstract* (1980, p. 882).

[e] 1972 or 1973.

[f] 1977.

Table A31. Science and Technology

	1950	1955	1960	1965	1970	1975	1979
Patent applications filed (thousands)[a]	—	—	82[g]	93[g]	101[g]	108	109
Outlays for research and development (billions of constant 1972 dollars)[b]	—	10	20	27	28	28	33
Number of scientists and engineers employed in research and development (thousands)[c]	—	237	426	495	546	535	630
Graduate enrollments in science fields (thousands)[d]	—	—	121	195	252	262	—
Science doctorates conferred (thousands)[e]	—	—	6	10	18	18	17
Engineering enrollments in institutions of higher education (thousands)[f]	180	242	270	309	316	310	394[g]

[a] U.S. Bureau of the Census, *Statistical Abstract of the United States* (1980, p. 572).

[b] *Statistical Abstract* (1980, p. 622).

[c] *Statistical Abstract* (1980, p. 627).

[d] *Statistical Abstract* (1980, p. 629).

[e] *Statistical Abstract* (1980, p. 629).

[f] National Center for Education Statistics, *Digest of Education Statistics* (1980, p. 94).

[g] 1978.

Table A32. Selected Indicators Relating to Inequality for Minorities

	1950	1955	1960	1965	1970	1975	1979
Life expectancy at birth[a]							
White	69.1	70.5	70.6	71.0	71.7	73.2	74.0[e]
Black and other	60.8	63.7	63.6	64.1	65.3	67.9	69.2[e]
Percentage of population 25 years old and over completing[b]							
High school							
White	—	—	25.8%	—	35.2%	37.3%	37.6%
Black	—	—	12.9	—	23.4	27.1	30.0
Spanish origin	—	—	—	—	—	23.0	25.6
College							
White	—	—	8.1	—	11.6	14.5	17.2
Black	—	—	3.1	—	4.5	6.4	7.9
Spanish origin	—	—	—	—	—	6.4	6.7
Percentage of voting age population registered in 11 Southern states, by race[c]							
White	—	—	62%	—	—	68%[f]	—
Black	—	—	29	—	—	63[f]	—
Black elected officials, number	—	—	—	—	1,472	3,503	4,503[e]
Ratio of nonwhite to white income[d]	.52	.53	.55	.59	.65	.67	—

[a] U.S. Bureau of the Census, *Statistical Abstract of the United States* (1980, p. 72).

[b] *Statistical Abstract* (1980, p. 149).

[c] *Statistical Abstract* (1980, p. 514).

[d] For families and unrelated individuals; Blinder (1980, p. 460).

[e] 1978.

[f] 1976.

Appendix B

*Data on the Educational
Attainments of the
American People*

Table B1. School and College Enrollments by Subjects and by Programs

(a) Percentage distribution of school enrollments, by various subject areas, grades 7 through 12, 1972-73[a]

Nonvocational		*Vocational*	
English	19%	Business	5%
Health and physical education	17	Industrial arts	5
Social studies	15	Home economics	4
Mathematics	11	Other	1
Natural sciences	10		15
Music	5		
Art	4		
Foreign language	4		
	85		

(b) Percentage distribution of high school enrollments by type of program, 1972[b]

Academic or college preparatory	44%
Vocational-technical	24
General	32
	100

(c) Probable major field of study in college as reported by full-time freshmen, 1977[c]

Nonvocational		*Vocational*	
Arts and humanities	10%	Business	22%
Biological sciences	5	Education	9
Physical sciences	3	Engineering	9
Social sciences	8	Other professional and technical	20
	26	Other (assumed to be mainly vocational)	14
			74

(d) Bachelors' degrees awarded, by major fields, 1976-77[d]

Nonvocational		*Vocational*	
Social sciences	13%	Business	17%
Natural sciences	10	Education	16
Letters and foreign languages	7	Health professions	6
Psychology	5	Engineering	5
Interdisciplinary and other	4	Fine and applied arts	5
Total	39	Public affairs	4
		Communications	3
		Agriculture	2
		Home economics	2
		Other	1
		Total	61

Table B1 (Continued)

(e) Percentage distribution of college faculties, by major field of highest degree, 1972-73[e]

Nonvocational		*Vocational*	
Biological sciences	7%	Business	4%
Physical sciences	12	Education	15
Social sciences	12	Engineering	6
Fine arts	8	Health sciences	5
Humanities	18	Other professional and technical	
Total	57	fields	7
		Total	37
		Unknown	7
		Grand total	100%

(f) Participants in adult education, by type of program, 1975[f]

	Number (thousands)	Percentage
General education	3,518	18%
Occupational training	8,307	43
Community issues	1,699	9
Personal and family living	2,532	13
Social life and recreation	2,714	14
Other	552	3
Total	19,322	100
Minus duplication for participants who enrolled in more than one type of program	-2,263	
Total number of participants	17,059	

[a] National Center for Education Statistics, *Digest of Education Statistics* (1980, p. 51).
[b] *Digest* (1980, p. 68).
[c] *Digest* (1980, p. 94).
[d] *Digest* (1980, pp. 112-116).
[e] *Digest* (1980, p. 102).
[f] *Digest* (1980, p. 149).

Table B2. Adult Performance Levels, by Type of Skill or Knowledge
and by Formal Educational Attainment, 1975

	Severely limited functional competence	Able to function with minimal adequacy	Proficient	Total
By type of skill or knowledge:				
Occupational knowledge	19.1%	31.9%	49.0%	100.0%
Consumer economics	29.4	33.0	37.6	100.0
Government and law	25.8	26.2	48.0	100.0
Health	21.3	30.3	48.3	100.0
Community resources	22.6	26.0	51.4	100.0
Reading	21.7	32.2	46.1	100.0
Problem solving	28.0	23.4	48.5	100.0
Computation	32.9	26.3	40.8	100.0
Writing	16.4	25.5	58.1	100.0
Overall performance	19.7	33.9	46.3	100.0
By formal educational attainment:				
Less than 6 years	85.0	13.0	3.0	100.0
6–7 years	49.0	37.0	14.0	100.0
8–11 years	18.0	55.0	27.0	100.0
High school completed	11.0	37.0	52.0	100.0
Some college	9.0	27.0	64.0	100.0
College graduate and beyond	2.0	17.0	80.0	100.0
Overall performance	19.7	33.9	46.3	100.0

Note: In 1975, the Northcutt studies were transferred from the University of Texas to the American College Testing (ACT) Program. In a report of ACT, User's Guide: Adult APL Study (1981, pp. 51–53), scores were published generally confirming the results shown in this table.

Sources: Northcutt and others (1975); U.S. Department of Commerce (1977).

**Table B3. Mean Percentage of Persons of Ages 37 to 48 Responding
Correctly to Questions in Public Opinion Polls on Information
and Knowledge, by Level of Education**

	Number of tests	Eighth-grade education	High school graduates	College graduates	Total population (estimate)[a]
Domestic public figures	15	39%	60%	70%	54%
Domestic events	7	29	45	65	45
Foreign public figures	3	41	77	84	66
Foreign events	6	57	77	95	73
Civics	3	31	41	75	43
Vocabulary	6	36	64	77	56
Tools used by boilermaker	3	60	57	61	58
Duties of personnel director	3	32	61	82	54

Note: These public opinion polls were taken in the late 1960s.

[a] Computed by author using appropriate weights for each of the three categories of respondents.

Source: Hyman, Wright, and Reed (1975, pp. 132, 134, 141, 143, 146).

Table B4. Mean Percentage of Persons of Ages 37 to 48 Approving Liberal Statements Involving Human Rights, by Level of Education

	Eighth-grade educations	High school graduates	College graduates	Total population (estimate)[a]
Allow speech against religion	50%	73%	94%	69%
Allow speech for government ownership	72	80	96	80
Allow admitted Communist to teach in a college	33	26	62	35
Strongly oppose jailing without bail a radical suspected of inciting riot	13	9	48	17
Always allow minority to criticize governmental decisions favored by majority	63	66	93	70
Favor freedom for individuals to intermarry	36	60	96	58
Vote for well-qualified black for president nominated by their party	55	80	88	73
Allow legal abortion where family is too poor to support another child	9	56	71	42
Against death penalty for persons convicted of murder	48	33	36	39

Note: These surveys were taken during the early 1970s.

[a] Computed by the author using appropriate weights for each of the three categories of respondents.

Source: Hyman and Wright (1979, pp. 93–96, 106, 109, 116, 122, 125).

Table B5. Percentage of Persons Entering or Attending Higher Education, by Income or Socioeconomic Status of Families, Selected Years

a) College plans of high school seniors, 1974[a]

Income Class (thousands of dollars)	Percentage		
	Planning to Attend	May Attend	Do Not Plan to Attend
0- 9.9	31%	30%	39%
10-14.9	42	28	30
15-24.9	53	25	22
25 or more	69	19	11

b) College entrance rates, 1967[b]

Socioeconomic Status (SES)	Percentage Entering
Lowest SES	45%
Second SES	54
Third SES	63
Highest SES	71

c) Enrollment in postsecondary education of high school seniors, 1973[c]

Income Class (thousands of dollars)	Percentage Attending
0- 2.9	29%
3.0- 5.9	33
6.0- 7.4	35
7.5- 8.9	39
9.0-10.4	44
10.5-11.9	42
12.0-13.4	47
13.5-14.9	49
15.0-17.9	57
18.0 or more	66

d) Educational attainment of the high school class of 1972, by socioeconomic status, 1976[d]

Socioeconomic Status	Bachelor's Degree or Higher[e]	Some College	No Higher Education
Lowest SES	7%	30%	63%
Middle SES	15	40	46
Highest SES	35	50	15

e) Enrollment of dependent family members, 18-24 years old, by family income, 1977[f]

Family Income (1967 dollars)	Percentage of Persons Enrolled
0-$ 5,000	22.6%
5,000- 9,999	34.3
10,000- 14,999	46.4
15,000 and over	59.8
Not reported	35.5

Table B5 (Continued)

[a] U.S. Bureau of the Census, *Social Indicators* (1976, p. 298).
[b] *Social Indicators* (1973, p. 106).
[c] *Social Indicators* (1976, p. 300).
[d] National Center for Education Statistics, *The Condition of Education* (1978, p. 130).
[e] These percentages refer to those receiving degrees four years from high school graduation. The percentage eventually getting degrees would be much higher.
[f] U.S. Bureau of the Census, *Social Indicators III* (1980, p. 295).

Bibliography ✤✤✤✤

Advisory Commission on Intergovernmental Relations. *The Federal Role in the Federal System: The Dynamics of Growth*. Washington, D.C.: Advisory Commission on Intergovernmental Relations, March 1981.

Agresto, J. "Liberty, Virtue, and Republicanism, 1776–1789." *The Review of Politics*, October 1977, pp. 473–504.

Agresto, J. "The American Founders and the Character of Citizens." *Character*, February 1981, pp. 1–3.

American College Testing Program. *User's Guide: Adult APL Survey*. Iowa City, Iowa: American College Testing Program, 1981.

Archambault, R. D. (Ed.). *John Dewey on Education*. Chicago: University of Chicago Press, 1964.

Bailey, S. K. *The Purposes of Education*. Bloomington, Ind.: Foundation Monograph Series, Phi Delta Kappa, 1976.

Barnes, H. E. *The University as the New Church*. London: C. A. Watts, 1970.

Beck, M. "The Expanding Public Sector: Some Contrary Evidence." *National Tax Journal*, March 1976, pp. 15–21.

Bell, D. *The Reforming of General Education.* New York: Columbia University Press, 1966.

Blinder, A. S. "The Level and Distribution of Economic Well-Being." In M. Feldstein (Ed.), *The American Economy in Transition.* Chicago: University of Chicago Press, 1980.

Boorstin, D. J., *Democracy and Its Discontents: Reflections on Everyday America.* New York: Random House, 1971.

Botstein, L. "The Debate over the Draft: We Need a Fresh Approach." *Chronicle of Higher Education,* September 2, 1980, p. 72.

Bowen, H. R. "Complexity and Values." In H. R. Bowen (Ed.), *Freedom and Control in a Democratic Society.* New York: American Council of Life Insurance, 1976.

Bowen, H. R. *Investment in Learning: The Individual and Social Value of American Higher Education.* San Francisco: Jossey-Bass, 1977.

Bowen, H. R. "Linking the Liberal Arts and Professional Education." In H. B. Sagen (Ed.), *Career Preparation in the Independent Liberal Arts College.* Chicago: Associated Colleges of the Midwest, 1978.

Bowen, H. R. *Adult Learning, Higher Education, and the Economics of Unused Capacity.* New York: College Entrance Examination Board, 1980a.

Bowen, H. R. *The Costs of Higher Education: How Much Do Colleges and Universities Spend per Student and How Much Should They Spend?* San Francisco: Jossey-Bass, 1980b.

Boyer, E. L., and Levine, A. *A Quest for Common Learning.* Washington, D.C.: The Carnegie Foundation for the Advancement of Teaching, 1981.

Brann, E.T.H. *Paradoxes of Education in a Republic.* Chicago: University of Chicago Press, 1979.

Breneman, D. W. "The Alternatives to Higher Education for Young People." Unpublished paper prepared for W. K. Kellogg Foundation, 1980.

Breneman, D. W., and Nelson, S. C. *Financing Community Colleges: An Educational Perspective.* Washington, D.C.: The Brookings Institution, 1981.

Broder, D. S. "The Moral Majority Could Change America's Face." *Los Angeles Times,* February 6, 1981.

Bronfenbrenner, U. "On Making Human Beings Human." *Character*, December 1980, p. 3.

Brown, B. F. (Ed.). *Education for Responsible Citizenship*. Report of the National Task Force on Citizenship Education. New York: McGraw-Hill, 1977.

Cahn, S. M. *Education and the Democratic Ideal*. Chicago: Nelson Hall, 1979.

Callahan, D., and Bok, S. (Eds.). *Ethics Teaching in Higher Education*. New York: Plenum Press, 1980.

Campbell, A. *The Sense of Well-Being in America: Recent Patterns and Trends*. New York: McGraw-Hill, 1981.

Carnegie Commission on Higher Education. *The Purposes and the Performance of Higher Education in the U.S. Approaching the Year 2000*. New York: McGraw-Hill, 1973.

Carnegie Council on Policy Studies in Higher Education. *Giving Youth a Better Chance: Options for Education, Work, and Service*. San Francisco: Jossey-Bass, 1980.

Charren, P. "Symposium on Television Entertainment." *Character*, November 1980, pp. 1–10.

Cheit, E. F. *The Useful Arts and the Liberal Tradition*. New York: McGraw-Hill, 1975.

Chickering, A. W. "Integrating Liberal Education, Work, and Human Development." *AAHE Bulletin*, March 1981, pp. 1–16.

Chronicle of Higher Education. "Voluntary Support for Colleges and Universities in 1979-80," May 18, 1981.

Clecak, P. *The Quest: American Paths to Self in the Sixties and Seventies*. New York: Oxford University Press, forthcoming.

Cleveland, H. "Forward to Basics: Education as Wide as the World." *Change*, May-June 1980, pp. 18–22.

Clinard, M. B., and Yeager, P. C. *Corporate Crime*. New York: Free Press, 1980.

Commission on the Humanities. *The Humanities in American Life*. Berkeley: University of California Press, 1980.

Counts, G. S. *Dare the School Build a New Social Order?* Carbondale: Southern Illinois University Press, 1978.

Cross, K. P. *Beyond the Open Door: New Students to Higher Education*. San Francisco: Jossey-Bass, 1971.

Cross, K. P. *Accent on Learning: Improving Instruction and Reshaping the Curriculum*. San Francisco: Jossey-Bass, 1976.

Crozier, M., Huntington, S. P., and Watanuki, J. *The Crisis of Democracy.* Report on the Governability of Democracies to the Trilateral Commission. New York: New York University Press, 1975.

Culley, J. F. (Ed.). *Contemporary Values and the Responsibility of the College.* Iowa City: College of Business Administration, University of Iowa, 1962.

Danziger, S. H., and Lampman, R. J. "Getting and Spending." In C. Taeuber (Ed.), *America in the Seventies: Some Social Indicators.* Philadelphia: *Annals of the American Academy of Political and Social Science,* January 1978, pp. 23–39.

Denison, E. F. "Effects of Selected Changes in the Institutional and Human Environment upon Output per Unit of Input." *Survey of Current Business,* January 1978, pp. 21–44.

Drucker, P. F. "Toward the Next Economics." *The Public Interest,* Special Issue, pp. 4–18.

Drucker, P. F. *The Changing World of the Executive.* New York: Times Books, forthcoming.

Durkheim, E. *Education and Sociology.* New York: Free Press, 1956.

Economic Report of the President. Washington, D.C.: U.S. Government Printing Office, annual.

Eddy, E. D., Jr. *The College Influence on Student Character.* Washington, D.C.: American Council on Education, 1959.

Educational Testing Service. *Moral Development.* Princeton, N.J.: Educational Testing Service, 1974.

Emmerij, L. *Can the School Build a New Social Order?* Amsterdam: Elsevier, 1974.

Eppley, G. "Reinstating the Draft: A Unique Opportunity." *Chronicle of Higher Education,* April 20, 1981, p. 29.

Exxon Corporation. *Dimensions 80.* New York: Exxon Corporation, 1981.

Feldstein, M. (Ed.). *The American Economy in Transition.* Chicago: University of Chicago Press, 1980.

Freeman, R. B., and Wise, D. A. *Youth Unemployment.* Cambridge, Mass.: National Bureau of Economic Research, 1979.

Gardner, J. W. *Morale.* New York: Norton, 1978.

Ginzberg, E. *Good Jobs, Bad Jobs, No Jobs.* Cambridge, Mass.: Harvard University Press, 1979.

Gleazer, E. G., Jr. *The Community Colleges: Values, Vision, and Vitality.* Washington, D.C.: American Association of Community and Junior Colleges, 1980.

Goldwin, R. A. (Ed.). *Higher Education and Modern Democracy.* Chicago: Rand McNally, 1967.

Grant, G., and Riesman, D. *The Perpetual Dream: Reform and Experiment in the American College.* Chicago: University of Chicago Press, 1978.

Grayson, C. J., Jr. "The U.S. Economy and Productivity: Where Do We Go from Here?" In U.S. Congress, Joint Economic Committee, *Special Study on Economic Change,* Vol. 10, December 29, 1980. Washington, D.C.: U.S. Government Printing Office, 1980.

Harris, L., and Associates. *The 1971 Reading Difficulty Index.* New York: Louis Harris and Associates, 1971.

Harvard Committee. *General Education in a Free Society.* Cambridge, Mass.: Harvard University Press, 1945.

Heard, A. *The Modern Culture of Higher Education: Many Missions and Nothing Sacred.* The Wilson Lecture. Nashville, Tenn.: Board of Higher Education, United Methodist Church, 1973.

Heilbroner, R. L., *An Inquiry into the Human Prospect.* New York: Norton, 1974.

Heller, W. W. "Economic Rays of Hope." *Wall Street Journal,* December 31, 1980a.

Heller, W. W. "Economic Policy for Inflation: Shadow, Substance, and Statistics." In *Reflections of America: Commemorating the Statistical Abstract Centennial.* Washington, D.C.: Bureau of the Census, U.S. Department of Commerce, 1980b.

Hirsch, F. *Social Limits to Growth.* Cambridge, Mass.: Harvard University Press, 1977.

Hunter, C. St. J., and Harman, D. *Adult Illiteracy in the United States.* New York: McGraw-Hill, 1979.

Hutchins, R. M. *The Higher Learning in America.* New Haven, Conn.: Yale University Press, 1936.

Hyman, H. H., and Wright, C. R. *Education's Lasting Influence on Values.* Chicago: University of Chicago Press, 1979.

Hyman, H. H., Wright, C. R., and Reed, J. S. *The Enduring Effects of Education.* Chicago: University of Chicago Press, 1975.

Johnston, L. D., Bachman, J. D., and O'Malley, P. M. *Monitoring the Future: Questionnaire Responses from the Nation's High School Seniors, 1979.* Ann Arbor: Survey Research Center, Institute for Social Research, University of Michigan, 1980.

Kaplan, M. (Ed.). *What Is an Educated Person?* New York: Praeger, 1980.

Kennan, G. F. "On the Nuclear Standoff and Its Insanity." *Los Angeles Times,* May 24, 1981, pp. IV-1, IV-2.

Kerr, C. "Higher Education: Paradise Lost?" Address given at Uppsala University, Uppsala, Sweden, September 28, 1977 (mimeograph).

Ketcham, R. *From Independence to Interdependence.* Princeton, N.J.: Aspen Institute for Humanistic Studies, 1976.

Keynes, J. M. "Economic Possibilities for Our Grandchildren." *Nation and Athenaeum,* October 11, 18, 1930. (Reprinted in *Essays in Persuasion.* London: Macmillan, 1972.)

Kibbee, R. J. *Quality and Equality in Higher Education.* New York: City University of New York, 1980. (Mimeograph.)

Kozol, J. *Prisoners of Silence.* New York: Continuum, 1980.

Kristol, I., and Weaver, P. H. (Eds.). *The Americans: 1976.* Lexington, Mass.: Lexington Books, 1976.

Landau, G. M. "Television." *Character,* January 1981, p. 5.

Lerner, M. *Values in Education.* Bloomington, Ind.: Phi Delta Kappa Educational Foundation, 1976.

Levine, A. *When Dreams and Heroes Died: A Portrait of Today's College Student.* San Francisco: Jossey-Bass, 1980.

Lippman, W. "The University." *The New Republic,* May 28, 1966, pp. 17-20.

Lipset, S. M. (Ed.). *The Third Centry: America as a Post-Industrial Society.* Stanford, Calif.: Hoover Institution Press, 1979.

Lyman, R. W. "What Kind of Society Should We Have?" *AAHE Bulletin,* December 1980, pp. 9-11.

McBee, M. L. (Ed.). *New Directions for Higher Education: Rethinking College Responsibilities for Values,* no. 31. San Francisco: Jossey-Bass, 1980.

McGrath, E. J. *Values, Liberal Education, and National Destiny.* Indianapolis: Lilly Endowment, n.d. (circa 1974).

McGrath, E. J. *General Education and the Plight of Modern Man.* Indianpolis: Lilly Endowment, n.d. (circa 1975).

Martin, W. "The Birth of a Media Myth." *The Atlantic*, June 1981, pp. 7–16.

Mayville, W. V. "Changing Perspectives on the Urban College and University." *AAHE/ERIC Higher Education*, April 1980.

Miller, D. E., and Orr, J. B. "Beyond the Relativism Myth." *Change*, October 1980, pp. 11–15.

Moberly, W. *The Crisis in the University.* London: SCM Press, 1949.

Morrill, R. L. *Teaching Values in College: Facilitating Development of Ethical, Moral, and Value Awareness in Students.* San Francisco: Jossey-Bass, 1980.

Muller, S. "Youth Service Deserves Examination." *Times Higher Education Supplement* (London), May 12, 1978.

Muscatine, C., and others. *Education at Berkeley.* Berkeley: University of California, 1966.

National Center for Education Statistics, U.S. Department of Education. *The Condition of Education.* Washington, D.C.: U.S. Superintendent of Documents, annual.

National Center for Education Statistics, U.S. Department of Education. *Digest of Education Statistics.* Washington, D.C.: U.S. Government Printing Office, annual.

National Center for Education Statistics, U.S. Department of Education. *Projections of Education Statistics to 1986–87.* Washington, D.C.: U.S. Superintendent of Documents, annual.

National Science Foundation. *Expenditures for Scientific Activities at Universities and Colleges, Fiscal Year 1977.* NSF 78-311. Washington, D.C.: National Science Foundation, 1977.

Newman, J. H. *The Scope and Nature of University Education.* New York: Dutton, 1958. (Originally published 1859.)

Niebuhr, H., Jr. *A Renewal Strategy for Higher Education.* Philadelphia: Temple University, 1979. (Mimeograph.)

Northcutt, N., and others. *Adult Functional Competency: A Summary.* Austin: University of Texas, 1975.

O'Toole, J. *Work, Learning, and the American Future.* San Francisco: Jossey-Bass, 1977.

Pace, C. R. *Education and Evangelism.* New York: McGraw-Hill, 1972.

Pace, C. R. *The Demise of Diversity.* New York: McGraw-Hill, 1974.

Pace, C. R. *Measuring Outcomes of College: Fifty Years of Findings and Recommendations for the Future.* San Francisco: Jossey-Bass, 1979.

Phenix, P. H. *Education and the Common Good.* New York: Harper & Row, 1961.

Pifer, A. "The Trends of the 1980s: Where Are They Leading Us?" Address to the Federation of Protestant Welfare Agencies, New York, April 2, 1981.

Plato. *The Republic.* (D. Lee, Trans.) (2nd ed.) New York: Penguin Books, 1974.

Premfors, R.I.T. *How Much Higher Education Is Enough? Public Policy in France, Sweden, and the United Kingdom.* New Haven, Conn.: Institute for Social and Policy Studies, 1979.

President's Commission for a National Agenda for the Eighties. *Government and the Advancement of Social Justice: Health, Welfare, Education, and Civil Rights in the Eighties.* Washington, D.C.: U.S. Government Printing Office, 1980a.

President's Commission for a National Agenda for the Eighties. *The Quality of American Life in the Eighties.* Washington, D.C.: U.S. Government Printing Office, 1980b.

President's Commission on Foreign Languages and International Studies. *Report of the President's Commission on Foreign Languages and International Studies.* Washington, D.C.: U.S. Government Printing Office, 1979.

President's Commission on Higher Education. *Higher Education for American Democracy.* New York: Harper & Row, 1947.

President's Commission on National Goals. *Goals for Americans.* Englewood Cliffs, N.J.: Prentice-Hall, 1960.

Ravitch, D. "Educational Policies That Frustrate Character Development." *Character,* July 1980, pp. 1–4.

Rawls, J. *A Theory of Justice.* Cambridge, Mass.: Harvard University Press, 1978.

Riesman, D. *On Higher Education: The Academic Enterprise in an Era of Rising Student Consumerism.* San Francisco: Jossey-Bass, 1980.

Ripley, F. C. "Postwar Trends in the Uses of National Output—A GNP Budget Approach." In U.S. Congress, Joint Economic

Committee, *Special Study on Economic Change*, Vol. 6, December 23, 1980.

Robert Johnston Company, Inc. *The Teen Environment*. Stamford, Conn.: Junior Achievement Inc., 1980.

Rockefeller, J. D., III. *The Second American Revolution*. New York: Harper & Row, 1973.

Saxon, D. S. "A Role for Universities in Ending the Arms Race." *Chronicle of Higher Education*, July 6, 1981, p. 48.

Schumacher, E. F. *Small is Beautiful*. New York: Harper & Row, 1973.

Seidman, P. "Public Safety: Crime Is Up But What About Punishment?" In C. Taeuber (Ed.), *America in the Seventies: Some Social Indicators*. Philadelphia: *Annals of the American Academy of Political and Social Science*, January 1978, pp. 248–267.

Smith, A. (R. H. Campbell, A. S. Skinner, and W. B. Todd, Eds.) *An Inquiry into the Nature and Causes of the Wealth of Nations*. Oxford: Clarendon Press, 1976. (Originally published 1776.)

Steinfels, P. *The Neoconservatives: The Men Who Are Changing American Politics*. New York: Simon & Schuster, 1979.

Stoddard, G. D. "Educating People for Outdoor Recreation." *The Circle of Omicron Delta Kappa*, Winter 1962-1963, pp. 1, 3.

Strauss, L. "Liberal Education and Mass Democracy." In R. A. Goldwin, *Higher Education and Modern Democracy*. Chicago: Rand McNally, 1965.

Taeuber, C. (Ed.). *America in the Seventies: Some Social Indicators*. Philadelphia: *Annals of the American Academy of Political and Social Science*, January 1978.

Ulich, R. *Three Thousand Years of Educational Wisdom*. (2nd ed.) Cambridge, Mass.: Harvard University Press, 1954.

U.S. Bureau of the Census. *Historical Statistics of the United States*. Washington, D.C.: U.S. Government Printing Office, 1975.

U.S. Bureau of the Census. *Social Indicators III: Selected Data on Social Conditions and Trends in the United States*. Washington, D.C.: U.S. Government Printing Office, 1980.

U.S. Bureau of the Census. *Statistical Abstract of the United States*. Washington, D.C.: U.S. Government Printing Office, annual.

U.S. Commission on Civil Rights. *Social Indicators of Equality for Minorities and Women*. Washington, D.C.: U.S. Commission on Civil Rights, 1978.

U.S. Department of Commerce, Office of Federal Statistical Policy and Standards and Bureau of the Census. *Social Indicators 1976.* Washington, D.C.: U.S. Government Printing Office, 1977.

U.S. Executive Office of the President, Office of Management and Budget. *Social Indicators, 1973.* Washington, D.C.: U.S. Government Printing Office, 1973.

Van Doren, M. *Liberal Education.* Boston: Beacon Press, 1959.

Veblen, T. *The Higher Learning in America.* New York: B. W. Heubsch, 1918.

Watkins, B. T. "Education Found Unused by Adults Who Need It Most." *Chronicle of Higher Education,* December 15, 1980, p. 6.

Wells, H. G. *The Outline of History.* New York: P. F. Collier, 1925.

White, G. "National Youth Service and Higher Education." Working paper, Sloan Commission on Government and Higher Education, October 1978.

Whitehead, A. N. *Aims of Education.* New York: Macmillan, 1929.

Wilson, R. W., Feldman, J. J., and Kovar, M. G. "Continuing Trends in Health and Health Care." In C. Taeuber (Ed.), *America in the Seventies: Some Social Indicators.* Philadelphia: *Annals of the American Academy of Political and Social Science,* January 1978, pp. 140–156.

Wirtz, W. *The Boundless Resource.* Washington, D.C.: New Republic, 1975.

Witmer, D. R. "Shall We Continue to Pursue Universal Higher Education?" In L. C. Solmon (Ed.), *New Directions for Education, Work and Careers: Reassessing the Link Between Work and Education, no. 1.* San Francisco: Jossey-Bass, 1978.

Yale College. *Report of the Study Group.* New Haven, Conn.: Yale University, 1972.

Index

A

Access, as goal, 2–3
Adams, J., 74
Adler, M., 117–118
Adult Performance Level Study, 18–19, 190
Advisory Commission on Intergovernmental Relations, 170*n*, 195
Agresto, J., 72, 74, 77, 84, 195
Alaska, college attendance in, 115
Alcoholism: problems of, 60; and progress, 41–42
American College Testing Program, 114, 190*n*, 195
American Council of Life Insurance, 69*n*
Archambault, R. D., 24, 82, 94, 195
Aristotle, 1, 96, 140
Arkansas, college attendance in, 115
Arnold, M., 96, 140
Arts: data on, 184; progress in, 45
Association of American Colleges, 96, 141
Astin, A., 11

Attainment, educational: analysis of, 11–23; conclusions on, 22–23; and content of education, 16–17; data on, 183, 187–194; periodic survey of, needed, 20–22; projections of, 13–16; studies of, 17–20; trends in, 12–13
Australia: gross domestic product of, 30; progress in, 27
Autonomy: of institutions, 5–6; provisions for, 83–84

B

Baccalaureate degree: and educated people, 102–104; modal concept of, 102–103
Bachman, J. D., 42, 59, 68*n*, 200
Bacon, F., 140
Bailey, S. K., 78, 151, 195
Barnes, H. E., 195
Beck, M., 30, 195
Bell, D., 141, 196
Berea College, as model, 147
Blinder, A. S., 186*n*, 196

205

Block, J. H., 118
Bloom, B., 118
Bok, S., 141, 197
Boorstin, D. J., 196
Botstein, L., 149n, 196
Bouwsma, W. J., 24, 103
Bowen, H. R., 6, 7, 17, 37, 69n, 86, 88, 94, 97, 100, 104, 110, 120, 125–126, 132, 155, 196
Boyer, E. L., xii, 121, 141, 196
Brann, E.T.H., 141, 196
Breneman, D. W., 128, 148, 196
Broder, D. S., 49, 196
Bronfenbrenner, U., 27, 197
Brown, B. F., 78, 197

C

Cahn, S. M., 197
California, college attendance in, 115
California, University of (Berkeley), Academic Senate report from, 141
Callahan, D., 141, 197
Campbell, A., 197
Campus environment, and values education, 137–139
Carlyle, T., 101
Carnegie Commission on Higher Education, 141, 197
Carnegie Council on Policy Studies in Higher Education, 143–145, 148, 197
Carnegie Foundation for the Advancement of Teaching, xii
Carroll, J., 118
Carter, J. E., 65
Charren, P., 197
Cheit, E. F., 104, 141, 197
Chickering, A. W., 104, 197
Church, and values, 78–79, 83–84
Churchill, W., 124
Clecak, P., 49–50, 197
Cleveland, H., 151, 153, 197
Clinard, M. B., 59, 197
College attendance: data on, 182, 188–189; differential rates of, 115, 193–194
College Board, 114

Comenius, J. A., 140
Commission on the Humanities, 197
Communications: data on, 181; progress in, 43–44
Community colleges, and youth, 147–148
Competence: data on, 190; studies of, 17–19
Comprehensive Employment and Training Act (CETA), 148
Computers, and equilibrium, 72–73
Confucius, 140
Counts, G. S., 197
Course content, and values education, 134–136
Course of study, for educated people, 104–108
Crime: data on, 179–180; problem of, 59; progress in, 42–43
Cross, K. P., 116, 197
Crozier, M., 197
Culley, J. F., 197
Curriculum: proliferation of, 5; and values education, 133–134

D

Danziger, S. H., 172n, 197
Democracy: analysis of education's role in, 69–81; conclusions on, 81; equilibrium in, 70–73
Denison, E. F., 37, 197
Dewey, J., 8, 24, 81, 82, 94, 96, 140
Discrimination, and progress, 46–47
Drucker, P. F., 129–130, 197
Drug abuse: problems of, 60; and progress, 41–42
Drug Enforcement Administration, 41
Durkheim, E., 198

E

Economy: and conditions of work, 35–36; and distribution of income, 36; equilibrium in, 70–71; higher education effects on, 123; and inflation, 36–37; and labor force, 31-33; and physical environment, 33-35; problems in, 55-59; problems in, as not permanent, ix; and production, 29-31; progress in, 29-37; as source of values, 84; and standard of living, 33; and values, 73-74

Eddy, E. D., Jr., 198

Educability: analysis of, 112-120; and diversity among learners, 116-119

Educated people: analysis of nation of, 99-124; and baccalaureate degree, 102-104; characteristics of, 108-112; characteristics of nation of, 120-124; concept of, 101-102; course of study for, 104-108; and educability, 112-120; and higher education, 99-124, 126-130; as informed and socially responsible, 66-67; negative effects of, 123-124; and values, 134

Education: analysis of role of, in democracy, 69-81; benefits of, 100; data on, 182-183; development of, 99-102; economic trends linked to, x; moral grounds for, 100-101; problems in, 60-64; progress in, 44-45; work integrated with, 148-149. *See also* Higher education

Education Amendments of 1980, Title XI of, 147

Education Commission of the States, 19*n*

Educational attainment. *See* Attainment, educational

Educational Testing Service, 86, 198

Eisenhower, D. D., 65

Emerson, R. W., 140

Emmerij, L., 198

Energy: data on, 168; progress in, 34

Environment: campus, and values education, 137-139; global, and progress, 50-51; physical, progress in, 33-35, 168-170; problem of, 57-59

Epictetus, 24

Eppley, G., 149*n*, 198

Equilibrium: and computers, 72-73; in democracy, 70-73

Erasmus, 140

Excellence, ideal of, 88

Extracurriculum, and values, 138

Exxon Corporation, 198

F

Faculty: compensation of, 7-8; interests and aspirations of, 5; and values education, 136-137, 138

Family: data on, 176; and educability, 113-114; problems of, 60-61; progress in, 38-40; and values, 61, 78, 83-84

Feldman, J. J., 40

Feldstein, M., 157, 158

Financing, and internal integrity, 96-97

Free mind: as higher education outcome, 121-122; ideal of, 86

Freeman, R. B., 198

G

Gardner, J. W., 119, 198

Georgia, college attendance in, 115

GI Bill of Rights, 2, 90, 114

Ginzberg, E., 198

Gleazer, E. G., Jr., 148, 199

Goldwin, R. A., 199

Governance: diffusion of control in, 89-90; and governmental authorities, 97; and internal integrity, 96-97

Government: equilibrium in, 71-72; as source of values, 84. *See also* Politics

Grant, G., 8, 199

Gray, T., 100-101

Grayson, C. J., Jr., 159*n*, 199

Gross national product, progress in, 29-30, 160-161

H

Harman, D., 18-19, 199

Harris, L., 18*n*, 199

208 Index

Harvard Committee, 141, 199
Health. *See* Longevity and health
Heard, A., 70, 199
Hedonism: and mass media, 62-63; rise of, 48-50
Height and weight, progress in, 40-41
Heilbroner, R. L., 199
Heller, W. W., 30, 56, 199
Higher education: agenda for, 125-155; challenges to, 67, 68; and and change in values, 78-80, 94, 132; changes in, resulting from growth, 4-8; conclusions on, 154-155; and cultural heritage, 122; and education for values, 130-141; ethos of, 86-88; future of, 8-10; goals of, 2-3; governance of, 89-90, 96-97; growth of, concentration on, 2-4; historical development of, 1-10; ideal of, 91; ideals refurbished for, 94-98; influential factors in, 85-91; and international reconciliation, 150-154; issues in, 9; moral authority of, 88-89; and nation of educated people, 99-124; 126-130; outcomes of, 11-23, 121-123; outside pressures on, 90; responsibilities of, for youth, 145-147; role of, 1-2, 10, 55; and social change, 82-98; as source of values, 83-85; strengths of, 95; as system, 90-91; values in, 69-81, 130-141; values different in, 93-94; and youth, 141-149. *See also* Education; Institutions
Hirsch, F., 33, 199
Humane values: as higher education outcome, 122; ideal of, 87
Hunter, C. St. J., 18-19, 199
Huntington, S. P., 197
Hutchins, R. M., 93, 117, 119, 141, 199
Hyman, H. H., 20, 132, 191n, 192n, 199

I

Illiteracy, extent of, 18-19
Income distribution: data on, 172-173; progress in, 36
Individuality, ideal of, 86-87
Inflation: data on, 173; problem of, 55-56; progress in, 36-37
Institutions: autonomy of, changes in, 5-6; elite, as models, 97-98; growth of, differential, 4; innovations by, 8; political control of, 5-6; private, and values education, 139-140; residential, for disadvantaged urban youth, 147. *See also* Higher education
International reconciliation: foreign studies for, tiers of, 152-153; and higher education, 150-154; and world community, 153-154
Investment, international, data on, 161

J

Jackson, A., 47
James, W., 27
Japan, gross domestic product of, 30
Jefferson, T., 47, 81, 140
Jesus, 78
John XXIII, Pope, 46
Johnson, L. B., 47
Johnston, L. D., 42, 59, 68n, 200

K

Kagan, J., 118
Kaplan, M., 24, 54, 89, 103, 117, 118, 141, 200
Kennan, G. F., 65-66, 200
Kennedy, J. F., 46, 47
Kentucky, college attendance in, 115
Kerr, C., 110, 125, 200

Ketcham, R., 76, 200
Keynes, J. M., ix–x, 200
Kibbee, R. J., 200
Knowledge: data on, 191; studies of, 19–20
Kovar, M. G., 40
Kozol, J., 18n, 200
Kristol, I., 87, 200

L

Labor force: data on, 162–163; progress in, 31–33; by sex, 32, 162; by type of work, 32–33, 163
Lampman, R. J., 172n, 197
Landau, G. M., 63, 200
Leadership, ideal of, 87
Lerner, M., 47, 119, 141, 200
Levine, A., 121, 141, 196, 200
Liberal learning: appreciation for, by students, 97; centrality of, 92–94; changes in, 92–93; and faculty development, 97; purpose of, 79; revival of, 79–80. *See also* Personal education, course of study for
Liberty, assumptions of, 82–83
Lincoln, A., 2
Lippman, W., 69, 200
Lipset, S. M., 200
Longevity and health: data on, 177–178; progress in, 40
Louisiana, college attendance in, 115
Luther, M., 113, 140
Lyman, R. W., 200

M

McBee, M. L., 200
McGrath, E. J., 118, 141, 200–201
Marriage, progress in, 39, 176
Martin, W., 49, 201
Marx, K., 78
Massachusetts, college attendance in, 115
Mayville, W. V., 147, 201

Media, mass: problems of, 62–64; and values, 62–63, 78, 83
Meiklejohn, A., 118
Michigan, University of, Survey Research Center of, 42
Mill, J. S., 96, 140
Miller, D. E., 86, 136, 201
Milton, J., 96, 140
Minorities: data on, 186; progress of, 46–47
Moberly, W., 141, 201
Morrill, R. L., 131, 141, 201
Muller, S., 149n, 201
Muscatine, C., 141, 201

N

Nation: achievements of, 51–52; characteristics of, if well-educated, 120–124; of educated people, 99–124, 126–130; pessimism about, 25–26; problems of, 54–68; progress of, 24–53
National Assessment of Educational Progress, 19–20
National Center for Education Statistics, 4n, 14n, 157, 182n, 185n, 189n, 194n, 201
National Institute of Alcohol Abuse and Alcoholism, 42
National Science Foundation, 4n, 201
National youth service, 149
Nelson, S. C., 148, 196
New Jersey, college attendance in, 115
New York, college attendance in, 115
Newman, J. H., 8, 96, 110–111, 140, 201
Niebuhr, H., Jr., 90, 201
Northcutt, N., 17–19, 190n, 201

O

Ogilvy, D., 44
O'Malley, P. M., 42, 59, 68n, 200
Orr, J. B., 86, 136, 201
O'Toole, J., 201
Ozarks, School of the, as model, 147

P

Pace, C. R., 17, 201-202
Patriotism, idea of, 66
Perkins, J. A., 152
Personal education, course of study for, 104-108
Pestalozzi, J. H., 140
Phenix, P. H., 108n, 141, 202
Philanthropy: data on, 175; progress in, 38
Philosophy, educational, increased attention to, 95-96
Piaget, J., 96
Pifer, A., 51, 53, 202
Plato, 70, 81, 82, 96, 110, 140, 202
Politics: maladies in, 75-76; problems in, 64-66; and values, 74-76. *See also* Government
Pollution: data on, 169-170; progress in, 35
Population: by age, 28; data on, 158; in metropolitan areas, 28-29; progress in, 28-29
Practical education, course of study for, 104-108
Premfors, R.I.T., 112, 202
President's Commission on Foreign Languages and International Studies, 152, 202
President's Commission on Higher Education, 2, 113, 202
President's Commission for a National Agenda for the Eighties, 47n, 146, 202
President's Commission on National Goals, 202
Pressure groups, and problems, 64-65, 76
Problems: analysis of, 54-68; conclusions on, 66-68; in economy, 55-59; in education, 60-64; in politics, 64-66; in social conditions, 59-60
Production: data on, 159-161; progress in, 29-31
Progress: analysis of, 24-53; background of, 24-27; in communications, education, arts, and sciences, 43-45; conclusions on, 51-53; data on, 157-186; in economy, 29-37; in population, 28-29; qualifications in, 26-27; in quality of life, 46-51; in social conditions, 37-43; in voting, 44, 182

Q

Quality of life: and hedonism, 48-50; and human rights, 48; and personal freedom, 47-48; progress in, 46-51; and protection of workers and consumers, 48; of submerged groups, 46-47, 186

R

Ravitch, D., 202
Rawls, J., 94, 202
Reagan, R., 44
Reed, J. S., 20, 191n, 199
Religious interest, and progress, 49-50
Research. *See* Teaching and research
Research Triangle Institute, 42
Resource use and conservation: data on, 168; problem of, 57-59; progress in, 34-35
Responsibility, sense of, weak, 131-132
Rhode Island, college attendance in, 115
Riesman, D., 6, 8, 199, 202
Ripley, F. C., 165n, 202-203
Robert Johnston Company, 68n, 203
Rockefeller, J. D. III, 203
Roosevelt, F. D., 47
Roosevelt, T., 47
Rousseau, J. J., 140

S

Saxon, D. S., 203
School: and neighborhood, problems of, 61-62, 183; and values, 78-79, 83-84
Schorske, C., 89

Schumacher, E. F., 75, 203
Science and technology: data on, 185; progress in, 45
Seidman, P., 180n, 203
Sloan Commission on Government and Higher Education, 149n
Smith, A., 70-71, 76, 90, 203
Social conditions: and crime, 42-43; and drug addiction and alcoholism, 41-42; and the family, 38-40; and higher education, 82-98; and longevity and health, 40-41; problems of, 59-60; progress in, 37-43; and social welfare, 37-38
Social welfare: data on, 174-175; progress in, 37-38
Socrates, 70
Standard of living: data on, 164-167; progress in, 33
Steinfels, P., 203
Stoddard, G. D., 203
Strauss, L., 64, 203
Students: changed characteristics of, 4-5; new, efforts for, 127-128; as peer group, and values, 138-139; potential, 128-129; power of, growth in, 6-7; role of, in institutional financing, 6; world perspectives for, 151-153
Surgeon General of the United States, 41, 68n
Switzerland, and nuclear shelters, 66

T

Taeuber, C., 157, 203
Teaching and research: influence of, 85-89; and youth problem, 146-147
Technology. See Science and technology
Texas, University of, 17, 99n
Tocqueville, A. de, 87
Trow, M., 86
Truman, H., 47
Trustees, boards of, 89-90

U

Ulich, R., 113, 203
Unemployment: data on, 162; problem of, 56-57; progress in, 31-32
U.S. Bureau of the Census, 4n, 12, 14n, 19, 28, 31n, 41, 57n, 157, 158n, 159n, 160n, 161n, 162n, 163n, 164n, 166n, 167n, 168n, 169n, 170n, 171n, 172n, 173n, 174n, 175n, 176n, 177n, 178n, 179n, 180n, 181n, 182n, 183n, 184n, 185n, 186n, 194n, 203
U.S. Commission on Civil Rights, 203
U.S. Department of Commerce, 190n, 204
U.S. Executive Office of the President, 204

V

Values: and campus environment, 137-139; cautions about, 133; change in, 78-80; concept of, 130; and course content, 134-136; and curriculum, 133-134; data on, 192; and economy, 73-74; and environmental deterioration and resource depletion, 58-59; and faculty, 136-137, 138; and family, 61, 78, 83-84; and higher education, 69-81, 130-141; and inflation, 56; literature on, 140-141; and mass media, 62-63, 78, 83; moral, system of, 131; and politics, 74-76; and pressure groups, 64-65; and private institutions, 139-140; quality of, 73-74; and social philosophy, 76-78; sources of, 83; studies of, 20, 191-192
Van Doren, M., 118, 141, 204
Veblen, T., 204
Vocational education: data on, 188-189; prominence of, 16-17; shift toward, 93. See also Practical education, course of study for
Voting: data on, 182; progress in, 44

W

War: and international reconcilia-
tion, 150–154; and problems, 65–
66
Watanuki, J., 197
Water, progress in, 34
Watkins, B. T., 128, 204
Weaver, P. H., 87, 200
Wells, H. G., 81, 120, 204
White, G., 149n, 204
Whitehead, A. N., 8, 106, 140, 204
Wilson, R. W., 40
Wilson, W., 47
Wirtz, W., 149, 204
Wise, D. A., 198
Witmer, D. R., 113, 204
Wordsworth, W., 103–104

Work, conditions of: data on, 171;
progress in, 35–36
Workplace, and values, 78
Wright, C. R., 20, 191n, 192n, 199

Y

Yale College, 204
Yeager, P. C., 59, 197
Youth: and crime, 59; and drug abuse
and alcoholism, 60; and family,
60–61; and higher education,
141–149; and mass media, 63;
plight of, 67–68; problems of,
141–143; and school and neighborhood, 61–62; typology of, 143–
144; and unemployment, 56–57;
and war, 65–66